JN277854

めざせ！**600点▶900点**

TOEIC®テスト
解いて覚える
英単語と
英熟語

リーディング
セクションの
問題を解く

**語彙力も
同時に
アップ！**

皇學館大学文学部講師
川村一代
Kazuyo Kawamura

こう書房

■■■ **はじめに** ■■■

　本書はTOEICのリーディングセクションのスコアを伸ばすための1冊です。タイトルにもあるように600点から900点レベルの問題を網羅しています。同時に、問題に出てくる語彙が頻出度によってランク付けされていますので、自分のレベルにあった学習が可能です。問題・語彙の両面から、600点から900点を目指す幅広い層のTOEIC受験者に使っていただける1冊です。

　本書の特徴として、「語彙力のアップ」に重点を置いたことがあげられます。タイトル『解いて覚える英単語と英熟語』が示すように、問題を解きながら同時に語彙力もアップさせるという意図のもとに、本書は執筆されました。語彙力は、言うまでもなくTOEIC受験において非常に重要な要素です。しかし単語をただ丸暗記するだけでは、本当に語彙力が身についたとは言えません。

　語彙学習には、意図的学習と付随的学習という2種類の方法があります。意図的学習とは、単語を暗記するなど意図的に語彙を学習することです。それに対して付随的学習とは、問題を解いたり本を読んだりする中で自然に単語を覚えていくという方法です。語彙学習において、短期的に語彙力をアップさせるには、意図的学習と付随的学習の組み合わせが効果的だとされています。本書では、両者をバランスよく組み合わせた学習ができるよう配慮しました。

　まず、「語彙のヒント」を見ずに問題を解いて下さい。問題文の中に知らない単語があれば、その意味を前後の文脈から推測してみて下さい。そして、そのあと、「語彙のヒント」で正しい意味を確認して下さ

い。これだけでもかなり効果はありますが、さらにその単語を暗記すれば、語彙力は確実にアップするでしょう。どの単語を暗記するかは、語彙のランク付けを参考に、自分のレベルにあったものを選んで下さい。余裕がある人は、「覚えてトクする語彙」も一緒に覚えると単語力倍増間違いなしです。

　リーディングセクション、とりわけ穴埋め問題はTOEICのスコアアップに即効性があります。本書は、TOEICに出やすい問題パターンをカバーしていますから、間違えた問題やカンで解いた問題は解説を読んで理解し、何日か日をおいて繰り返しトライしてみて下さい。

　読解問題は、先に述べた付随的語彙学習に効果的なセクションです。穴埋め問題と同様に、機械的に問題を解くだけでなく、単語の意味がわからないときは、前後の文脈から正しい意味を推測する練習をしてみて下さい。そして、「語彙のヒント」で推測した意味が正しかったかどうか答え合わせをしましょう。

　本書が、TOEICを受験者する皆さんの得点アップに役立つことを願ってやみません。本書を最大限活用して900点突破を目指して下さい。

　この本を上梓するにあたり、いろいろな方々にお世話になりました。皇學館大学John Dykes助教授、関西外国語大学短期大学部Shannon Black講師には、英文校閲の労を取っていただきました。また、編集の立場から、こう書房の鈴木啓一氏には絶えず適切なご助言と励ましをちょうだいしました。これらの方々にこの場を借りて、衷心より感謝の意を表したいと思います。

　2006年4月　　　　　　　　　　　　　　　　　　　　　　　　著者

CONTENTS

- はじめに … 1
- 新TOEICテストについて … 4
- 本書の使い方 … 6

- **第1章** パート5 **短文穴埋め問題** … 7
- **第2章** パート6 **長文穴埋め問題** … 119
- **第3章** パート7 **読解問題** … 141
  - 1つの文書 … 142
  - 2つの文書 … 182

- 索引 … 222

カバーデザイン　冨澤　崇（Ebranch）

■■■ 新TOEICテストについて ■■■

　TOEIC（Test of English for International Communication）は、英語によるコミュニケーション能力を測定するテストです。世界共通の英語能力認定試験として、世界最大の規模を誇る米国の教育研究機関 EST（Educational Testing Service）が開発・制作にあたり、約60ヶ国で、年間約450万人以上が受験しています。

　1972年12月の第1回公開テスト以来、日本国内において延べ1,300万人以上の人が受験したTOEICテストが、2006年5月実施の第122回公開テストより、リニューアルされることになりました。

　ESTでは、2004年に日本を含む世界11ヶ国の機関・企業の協力を得て、Global Surveyを実施し、現在働く環境の場でどのような英語能力が必要とされているのか調査・検証を行ないました。その結果をふまえ、実際のコミュニケーションで必要とされる英語能力を評価するために、より現実に即した状況や設定をテスト上でも再現されるよう改定されたのが新TOEICです。

　問題形式の具体的な変更は、以下の7点です。

＜リスニングセクション＞

❶ パート1の写真描写問題の削減。

❷ パート3、パート4の設問の音声化。

❸ パート3、パート4では各会話やトークなどに対して設問を3問ずつ設定。

❹ 米国・英国・カナダ・オーストラリア（ニュージーランドを含む）の発音を採用。各発音の出題の割合は25％ずつ。

<リーディングセクション>

❶ 旧TOEICテストのパート6、誤文訂正問題の削除。
❷ 新TOEICテストのパート5は短文の中の空所に単語を補充。パート6では長文の中に複数ある空所に単語を補充。
❸ 新TOEICテストのパート7では2つの文書を読んで設問に答える問題を追加。

　問題はリスニングセクション（45分間・100問）と、リーディングセクション（75分間・100問）からなり、2時間で200問に答えます。途中、休憩はありません。リスニングセクションはテープに吹き込まれた会話やナレーションを聞いて設問に答えます。リーディングセクションは印刷された問題を読んで答えます。

　リスニング・リーディングセクションとも5点〜495点で、トータル10点〜990点のスコアで5点刻みに表示されます。テストは英文のみで構成されたマークシート方式の一斉客観テストです。

　題材にはこれまでどおり、一般的な場面、またはビジネスでのコミュニケーションの場面が想定されており、特殊なビジネス英語の知識を必要としたり、特定の国の歴史や文化に関連する事象がわからなければ解答できない問題はありません。

　新TOEICテストでは、問題作成において、「より実際的な」というコンセプトが基本となっています。旧TOEICテストと比べて、問題文が若干長文化しているものの、英語コミュニケーション能力の測定という点では、旧TOEICも新TOEICも大きな違いはありません。具体的にどんな点が変更されたかをふまえ、その形式に慣れておけば、心配する必要はありません。今までと同様2時間という長いテスト時間ですが、集中力を欠かずに頑張れば、問題はないでしょう。

■■■ 本書の使い方 ■■■

本書には「一石二鳥、三鳥、四鳥…」のトクする学習を促進する他書には類を見ないユニークな学習プログラムが用いられています。ですから、必ず以下の指示に従って効率良く学習して下さい。

❶ Part 5, 6, 7の各問題は辞書などを使わず、まずは自力でチャレンジして下さい。

❷ 問題を解いた後は、問題のすぐ下にある **《語彙のヒント》** を参考にして、もう一度問題の正解が何になるのかを考えて下さい。ヒントとなる語（句）は基本的・標準的なものですから、発音記号とともに意味をしっかりとおさえて下さい。

❸ ここで答え合わせをします。解答・解説の部分を見て下さい。正解であっても、不正解であっても、日本語訳、解説の部分をよく読んで完全に理解できるようにして下さい。

❹ 次に **覚えてトクする語彙** の欄を見て下さい。ここには、各問題に出ている語彙の派生語、関連語、熟語などを載せています。TOEICによく出る語彙ばかりですので、できるだけ覚えるようにして下さい。

❺ Part 5, 6, 7の全問題を上記❶〜❹の要領で、一度だけでなく、何度も繰り返し学習することをお薦めします。一度の学習だけですべてが定着することはほとんどありません。語学学習には、Practice makes perfect.「習うより慣れろ」の実践が最も大切です。

❶〜❺の学習を徹底的に行なうことで、みなさんは必ずTOEICテスト600点はもちろんのこと、730点、860点のスコアを楽に突破し、900点でさえ突破できる実力を養成することができるでしょう。みなさんの健闘をお祈りします。

《語彙のヒント》 と **覚えてトクする語彙** の単語・熟語の横についている星印はTOEICテストにそれぞれの単語・熟語がどれだけ頻繁に出題されるかを表わすマーク（出る順マーク）です。掲載されている単語・熟語は、すべてTOEICテストによく出題されますが、さらに出題頻度順に３段階に分けました。それぞれ

　　★★★ 〜出題頻度が最も高い
　　★★★ 〜出題頻度がとても高い
　　★★★ 〜出題頻度が高い

を意味しています。

第1章

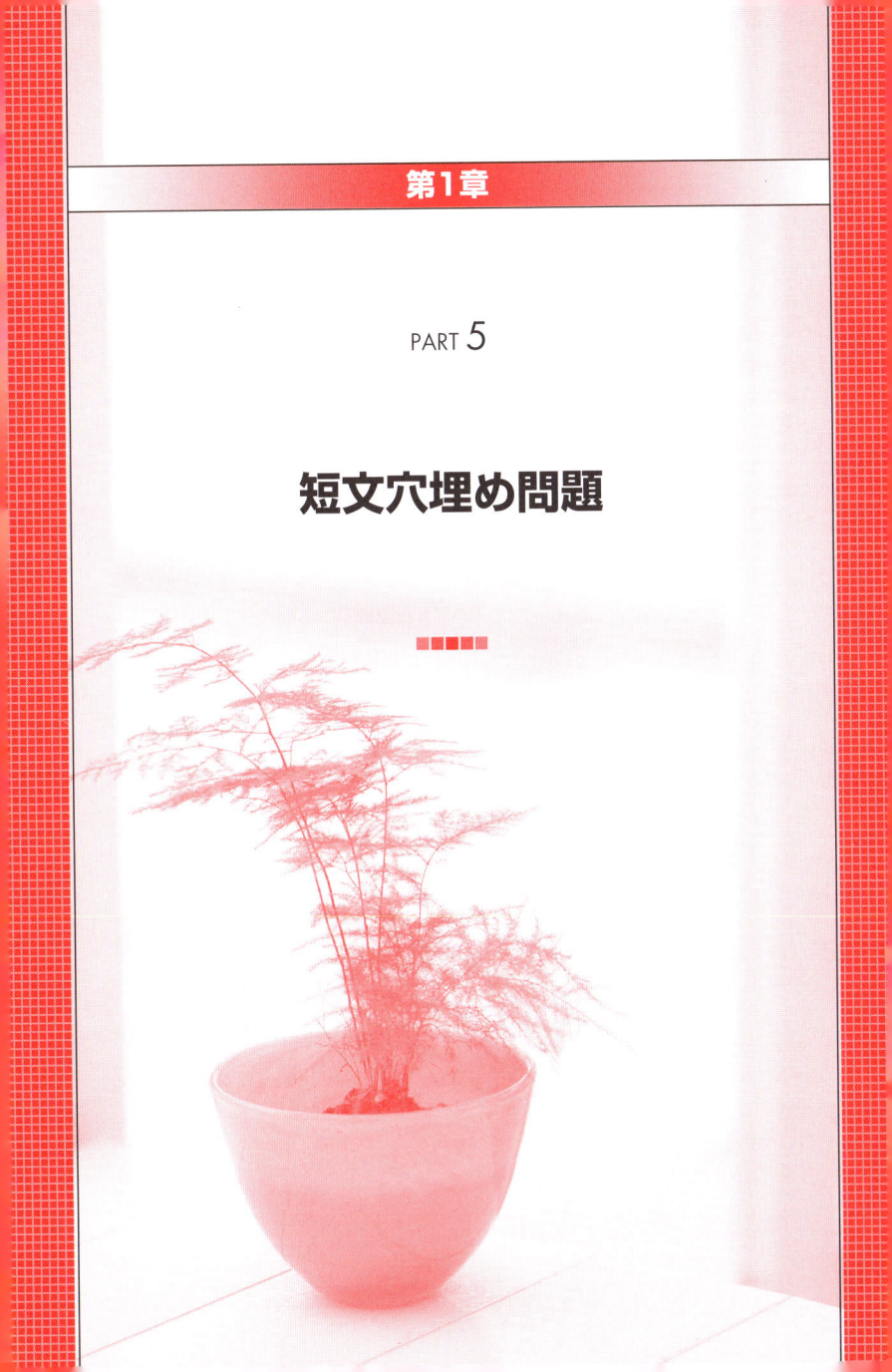

PART 5

短文穴埋め問題

001

Candidates selected for an interview will be ------- by someone from the interview committee.

(A) notice
(B) notified
(C) notifying
(D) notification

《語彙のヒント》

candidate 名 候補者、志願者 ★★★
[kǽndidèit]
select 動 …を選ぶ（ある目的のために最もふさわしいものを多数の中から選ぶ） ★★★
[səlékt]
committee 名 委員会 ★★★
[kəmíti]

002

Volunteers are needed to help take part ------- whale and dolphin research projects in Scotland, Italy and Greece.

(A) on
(B) at
(C) in
(D) with

《語彙のヒント》

volunteer 名 有志、ボランティア ★★★
[vὰləntíər]
whale 名 くじら ★★★
[hwéil]
project 名 事業、企画 動 …を予測する ★★★
[prάdʒəkt]

第1章 ● パート5 短文穴埋め問題

覚えてトクする語彙

presidential candidate 名 大統領候補 ★★★
job candidate 名 企業の採用候補者 ★★★
candid 形 包み隠しのない ★★★
Candid Camera 名 『どっきりカメラ』(隠し撮りのテレビ番組) ★★★
choose 動 …を選ぶ(一般的に、いくつかのものから特定のものを選ぶ) ★★★
selection 名 (よいものの)選択 ★★★
selective 形 えり抜きの ★★★
notice 動 …に気づく 名 通知 ★★★
commit 動 (権限など)を委託する、(罪など)を犯す ★★★
commitment 名 公約、献身 ★★★

解答・解説 answer and explanation

Answer (B) **Key Point** 受動態
面接に選ばれた候補者には、面接委員会から知らせがある。
解法 空欄の前後は be と by だから、空欄には受動態が入るという予測がつく。notify「…を通知する」を受動態に変えると notified となる。

覚えてトクする語彙

voluntary 形 自発的な、ボランティアの ★★★
voluntarily 副 自発的に ★★★
take in ~ 熟 …をだます、理解する、…に行く ★★★
take ~ in (one's) stride 熟 …を楽々とこなす ★★★
take up with ~ 熟 …と話し合う ★★★
whaler 名 捕鯨者、捕鯨船 ★★★
whaling 名 捕鯨、捕鯨業 ★★★
projector 名 投影機 ★★★
projection 名 投影 ★★★
projective 形 投影の ★★★

解答・解説 answer and explanation

Answer (C) **Key Point** 熟語、前置詞
スコットランド、イタリア、ギリシアでは、くじらとイルカの調査プロジェクトに参加するボランティアが必要とされている。
解法 take part in ~で「~に参加する」という熟語である。

003

Consumer prices ------- by 0.3 percent in January, the biggest one-month increase in nine months.

(A) rose
(B) risen
(C) raised
(D) arisen

《語彙のヒント》

consumer 名 顧客 ★★★
[kənsúːmər]
price 名 価格 ★★★
[práis]

004

The country's top wholesale food distributor slashed its fourth-quarter earnings -------.

(A) looking
(B) outlook
(C) overlook
(D) onlooking

《語彙のヒント》

wholesale 名 卸売り ★★★
[hóulsèil]
distributor 名 流通業者 ★★★
[distríbjutər]
slash 動 （予算など）を大幅削減する、…に深く切りつける ★★★
[slǽʃ]

第1章 ● パート5 短文穴埋め問題

覚えてトクする語彙

consumer price index 名 消費者物価指数 ★★★
consumption 名 消費 ★★★
consumption tax 名 消費税 ★★★
consume 動 …を消費する ★★★
consumable 形 消費できる 名《通常~s》消耗品 ★★★
consumedly 副 非常に ★★★
priceless 形 非常に貴重な ★★★
pricy 形 高価な ★★★
list price 名 定価（価格表に掲載されている値段） ★★★
unit price 名 セット価格 ★★★
at any price 熟 どんな犠牲を払っても ★★★

解答・解説

Answer (A) **Key Point**▶ 自動詞

消費者物価は1月に0.3％上がり、過去9ヶ月間での最大の増加だ。

解法▶ 自動詞 rise「上がる」と他動詞 raise「…を上げる」は、混同しやすいので、しっかり区別して記憶を確かなものにしよう。

覚えてトクする語彙

wholesaler 名 卸売り業者 ★★★
distribute 動 …を分配する ★★★
distribution 名 配分、分布 ★★★
quarter 名 四半期、4分の1 ★★★
earnings 名 収益、所得 ★★★
outfit 名 会社 ★★★
outlay 名 支出 ★★★
outplacement 名 再就職斡旋 ★★★
outright 形 完全な [áutrài] 副 完全に [àutráit] ★★★
outstanding 形 傑出した、未払いの ★★★

解答・解説

Answer (B) **Key Point**▶ 単語

その国で一番の食品卸売り業者は、第4四半期収益の見通しを大幅に削減した。

解法▶ fourth-quarter earnings「第4四半期収益」に続くので、(B) outlook「見通し」が文脈上適する。(C) overlook は「見過ごし」、(D) onlooking は「傍観している」という意味。

005

Dr. James D. Hardy was the surgeon who implanted the first animal heart ------- a human.

(A) on (B) off
(C) into (D) with

《語彙のヒント》

surgeon 名 外科医 ★★★
[sə́ːrdʒən]
implant 動 (臓器・皮膚など)を移植する、(思想・信条など)を植えつける ★★★
[implǽnt]

006

Michael Johnson will be assuming the new position of Director of Human Resources, ------- March 1.

(A) effect (B) affect
(C) effective (D) affective

《語彙のヒント》

assume 動 …を引き受ける、負う ★★★
[əsúːm]
human resources 名 人事、人材 ★★★
[hjùːmən risɔ́ːrsiz]

第1章 ● パート5 短文穴埋め問題

覚えてトクする語彙

surgery 名 手術 ★★★
plastic surgery 名 美容整形 ★★★
surgical 形 外科の ★★★
physician 名 医師、内科医 ★★★
dermatologist 名 皮膚科医 ★★★
gynecologist 名 産婦人科医 ★★★
pediatrician 名 小児科医 ★★★
anesthetist 名 麻酔医 ★★★
implantation 名 移植、教え(植え込む)こと ★★★
silicon implant 名 (豊胸手術での)シリコン注入 ★★★

解答・解説

Answer (C)　　　　　　　　　　　　　　　　　**Key Point** 熟語、前置詞

ジェームズ・D・ハーディ博士は、人間に動物の心臓を最初に移植した外科医だった。

解法→ implant A in [into] B で「A を B に移植する、植えつける」という意味である。

覚えてトクする語彙

assumption 名 仮定、就任 ★★★
assumable 形 仮定できる ★★★
assumably 副 おそらく ★★★
assuming 接 …と仮定して ★★★
in effect 熟 実質的には ★★★
take effect 熟 (法律などが)実施される ★★★
come into effect 熟 (法律などが)実施される ★★★
side effect 名 副作用 ★★★
affection 名 愛情 ★★★
affectionate 形 愛情のこもった ★★★

解答・解説

Answer (C)　　　　　　　　　　　　　　　　　**Key Point** 副詞

マイケル・ジョンソンは3月1日付けで新しい人事課長になる予定だ。

解法→ effective には、形容詞の「効果的な」という意味以外に、副詞の「(特定の日時)をもって」という意味もあるので再確認しておこう。(A) effect は名詞で「結果」、動詞で「…を結果としてもたらす」、(B) affect は「…に影響を及ぼす」、(D) affective は「感情の」という意味である。

007

Bond prices faded Friday as Wall Street stocks rose and ------- a second straight winning week.

(A) end
(B) ended
(C) ending
(D) to end

《語彙のヒント》

bond 名 公債 ★★★
[bánd]
fade 動 薄れる、衰える ★★★
[féid]
stock 名 株 ★★★
[sták]

008

A judge dismissed a lawsuit ------- video rental giant Movies Galore Inc. and five movie studios.

(A) to
(B) on
(C) for
(D) against

《語彙のヒント》

judge 名 裁判官 動 …を判断する ★★★
[dʒʌ́dʒ]
dismiss 動 …を棄却する ★★★
[dismís]
lawsuit 名 訴訟 ★★★
[lɔ́ːsùːt]

覚えてトクする語彙

corporate bonds 名 社債 ★★★
government bonds 名 国債 ★★★
bond certificate 名 債権 ★★★
fade in 熟 画面をしだいに明るくする、音量をしだいに大きくする ★★★
fade out 熟 画面をしだいに暗くする、音量をしだいに小さくする ★★★
stock certificate 名 株券 ★★★
stock dividend 名 株式配当 ★★★
stock exchange 名 株式取引所 ★★★
blue chips 名 優良銘柄、優良株 ★★★
gaining issues 名 値上がり株 ★★★

解答・解説 answer and explanation

Answer (B)　　　　　　　　　　　　　　　　　　　**Key Point** 並列

ウォール街の株価が上がって、2週連続利益増で終わったので、公債価格は金曜日に衰えた。
解法➡ as 以下の従属節内の主語は Wall Street stocks で、動詞は rose である。動詞 rose の後に並列の and があり、and の前後は品詞をそろえなければならない。したがって、空欄は動詞の過去形である (B) ended を選ぶ。

覚えてトクする語彙

judgment 名 判断 ★★★
judgmental 形 性急に判断を下しがちな ★★★
judicial 形 裁判の、司法の ★★★
judicious 形 判断力の確かな ★★★
dismissal 名 解雇 ★★★
law firm 名 法律事務所 ★★★
law school 名 ロースクール、法律大学院 ★★★
litigation 名 訴訟 ★★★
litigate 動 訴訟する ★★★
sue 動 …を訴える ★★★

解答・解説 answer and explanation

Answer (D)　　　　　　　　　　　　　　　　　　　**Key Point** 前置詞

裁判官は、ビデオレンタルの巨大企業ムービーズ・ガロア社と5つの映画スタジオに対する訴訟を棄却した。
解法➡ a lawsuit against ～で「…に対する訴訟」の意味である。

009

Underage drinkers account for nearly 20 percent of the alcohol ------- in the United States each year.

　　(A) assumed　　　　(B) consumed
　　(C) resumed　　　　(D) presumed

《語彙のヒント》

underage 形 必要な年齢に達しない、未成年の ★★★
[ʌ̀ndəréidʒ]
account 動 占める、説明する 名 理由、説明 ★★★
[əkáunt]

010

A former insurance broker ------- with scamming investors pleaded guilty to fraud in the midst of his trial.

　　(A) charge　　　　(B) charged
　　(C) charging　　　(D) to charge

《語彙のヒント》

scam 動 …をペテンにかける 名 ペテン、詐欺 ★★★
[skæm]
plead 動 …を申し立てる、主張する ★★★
[plíːd]
fraud 名 詐欺 ★★★
[frɔ́ːd]

第1章 ● パート5 短文穴埋め問題

覚えてトクする語彙

understaffed 形 人員が足りない ★★★
underlying 形 内在する ★★★
underway 形 進行中で ★★★
accountable 形 (説明の) 責任がある ★★★
accountability 名 (説明の) 責任 ★★★
resumption 名 再開 ★★★
résumé 名 履歴書 ★★★
presumption 名 推定、仮定 ★★★
presumable 形 推定できる、ありそうな ★★★
presumably 副 推定上 ★★★

解答・解説

Answer (B)　　　　　　　　　　　　　　　　**Key Point** 単語

毎年アメリカで消費されるアルコールの20%近くを、未成年の飲酒者が占めている。

解法 ➡ 「毎年アメリカで…アルコールの20%」という文脈から、(B) consumed 「消費される」が適切である。(A) assume 「…を仮定する」、(C) resume 「(仕事・話など) を再び始める」、(D) presume 「確信をもって…を推定する」は文脈上適さない。この場合の consumed は過去分詞であり、直前の alcohol を修飾している。

覚えてトクする語彙

insurant 名 非保険者、保険契約者 ★★★
insurer 名 保険業者、保険会社 ★★★
on the charge of ~ 熟 …の罪で ★★★
scamper 動 あわてて走り去る ★★★
scan 動 …をくわしく調べる、走り読みする ★★★
scar 名 傷跡 ★★★
plead guilty 熟 有罪を認める答弁をする ★★★
plea 名 弁解、(訴訟で事実の) 申し立て ★★★
pleabargain 動 司法取引する ★★★

解答・解説

Answer (B)　　　　　　　　　　　　　　　　**Key Point** 分詞

投資家をだましていたと告発された前保険仲介業者は、裁判の最中に詐欺罪を認めた。

解法 ➡ この文の主語は A former insurance broker で、動詞は pleaded であり、主語と動詞が存在するので、空欄には a former insurance broker を修飾する形容詞が入る。文脈上、「告発された」と受身にしなければならないので、charge 「…を告発する」の過去分詞形の (B) charged が正解。

011

Meat processor Smithfield Foods Inc. reported sharply lower earnings for its third quarter as sales ------- 4 percent.

(A) fall
(B) fell
(C) fallen
(D) falling

《語彙のヒント》

processor 名 加工業者、処理装置 ★★★
[prásesər]
report 動 …を発表する、公表する ★★★
[ripɔ́ːrt]

012

Language functions as a ------- of thinking, not to mention as a means of communication.

(A) mean
(B) means
(C) meaning
(D) meanings

《語彙のヒント》

language 名 言語 ★★★
[læŋgwidʒ]
function 動 作用する 名 機能 ★★★
[fʌ́ŋkʃən]
not to mention ~ 熟 …は言うまでもなく ★★★
[nɔt tə ménʃən]

第1章 ● パート5 短文穴埋め問題

覚えてトクする語彙

grinded meat 名 ひき肉 ★★★
meat-and-potatoes 名 主旨、基本 ★★★
word processor 名 ワープロ ★★★
food processor 名 フードプロセッサー ★★★
process 名 過程 動 …を処理する 自 列になって歩く ★★★
procession 名 行列、行進 ★★★
reportedly 副 伝えられるところによれば ★★★
report card 名 通信簿、成績表 ★★★

解答・解説

Answer (B)   *Key Point* ▶ 時制

食肉加工業者のスミス・フーズ社は、売り上げが4％落ちたため、第3四半期の収益が急に下がったと発表した。

解法➡ 接続詞 as の前に、主語(Meat processor Smithfield Foods Inc.)・動詞(reported)がそろった文があるので、as の後も、主語・動詞のそろった文が必要である。sales が主語なので、空欄には動詞が入る。前半が reported と過去形なので、fall「落ちる」の過去形 (B) fell が適切。

覚えてトクする語彙

language laboratory 名 語学演習室、LL教室 ★★★
languid 形 活気のない、けだるい ★★★
languish 動 (人・花が) しおれる ★★★
functional 形 機能上の、機能的な ★★★
by all means 熟 もちろんだとも、ぜひどうぞ ★★★
by no means 熟 決して…でない ★★★
by any means 熟 決して、どうしても ★★★
by means of ~ 熟 …を用いて ★★★
live within *one*'s means 熟 身分相応に暮らす ★★★
mention 動 …について言及する ★★★

解答・解説

Answer (B)   *Key Point* ▶ 単語

言語は、コミュニケーションの手段であることは言うまでもなく、思考の手段としても機能している。

解法➡ 「手段、方法」という意味の mean は、通常 s をつけて means で使われ、単数・複数両方の意味で使われる。as a means of ~「…の手段として」の形で覚えておくと便利。動詞 mean「…を意味する」の名詞形は、meaning「意味」である。

013

An Alabama company is recalling 72,000 boxes of sparklers ------- the handles can catch fire and disintegrate.

(A) because
(B) due to
(C) on account of
(D) because of

《語彙のヒント》

recall 動 …を回収する ★★★
[rikɔ́ːl]
sparkler 名 線香花火 ★★★
[spáːrklər]
disintegrate 動 分解する、崩壊する ★★★
[disíntəgrèit]

014

Most patients ------- for depression should remain on medication after their gloom has lifted.

(A) treat
(B) treated
(C) treating
(D) that treat

《語彙のヒント》

depression 名 うつ病、不景気 ★★★
[dipréʃən]
medication 名 投薬、薬物治療 ★★★
[mèdəkéiʃən]
gloom 名 憂うつ、暗闇 ★★★
[glúːm]

第1章 ● パート5 短文穴埋め問題

覚えてトクする語彙

sparkle [動] 火花を発する、輝く、泡立つ ★★★
sparkling [形] 輝く、活気のある、発泡性の ★★★
sparkling wine [名] スパークリングワイン ★★★
get a handle on ~ [熟] …を調べる、管理する ★★★
dismount [動] 自転車から降りる ★★★
disown [動] …を自分のものと認めない ★★★
discomfit [動] …を完敗させる、当惑させる ★★★
disburse [動] (基金から金) を支払う ★★★

解答・解説

Answer (A)　　　　　　　　　　　　　　**Key Point** 接続詞

あるアラバマの会社は、花火の柄の部分に火がついてばらばらになる可能性があるので、7万2000箱の線香花火を回収している。

解法➡ 空欄の前半は、主語 (An Alabama company) と動詞 (is recalling) が存在する文であり、後半も、主語 (the handles) と動詞 (can catch) が存在する文である。したがって、文と文をつなぐには、接続詞が必要である。(A) because 以外の選択肢は、2語以上からなり、前置詞の役割を持つ群前置詞である。

覚えてトクする語彙

treatment [名] 治療 ★★★
depressed [形] 意気消沈した、不景気の ★★★
medicate [動] …を薬で治療する ★★★
Medicare [名] メディケア (65歳以上の人や身体障害者などに対するアメリカの医療保険制度) ★★★
Medicaid [名] メディケイド (低所得者に対するアメリカの医療扶助制度) ★★★
gloomy [形] 憂うつな、暗い ★★★
lift a hand [finger] [熟] ほんの少し骨を折る ★★★

解答・解説

Answer (B)　　　　　　　　　　　　　　**Key Point** 分詞

うつ病の治療を受けているほとんどの患者は、うつ状態が去った後も、薬物治療を続けるべきである。

解法➡ 問題文にはすでに動詞 should remain が存在する。よって、空欄に動詞は入らない。空欄は most patients を修飾する形容詞となる過去分詞を入れる。ほとんどの患者は治療を「した」のではなく「受けている」のだから、(B) treated が正解である。treat は「…を治療する」を意味する動詞である。

015

The new owner of Sunrise Brewing Co. is replacing Patrick Dilger as president of the second ------- U.S. brewery.

(A) large
(B) larger
(C) largest
(D) most large

《語彙のヒント》

owner 名 所有者 ★★★
[óunər]
replace 動 …に取って代わる ★★★
[ripléis]
brewery 名 (ビールなどの) 醸造所 ★★★
[brú:əri]

016

Many people begin the day by checking news websites, ------- them as a kind of surrogate newspaper.

(A) used
(B) using
(C) to use
(D) being used

《語彙のヒント》

website 名 ウエブサイト、ワールドワイドウエブの情報サイト ★★★
[wébsàit]
surrogate 形 代理の 名 代行者 ★★★
[sə́:rəgèit]

第1章 ● パート5 短文穴埋め問題

覚えてトクする語彙

own 動 …を所有する 形 自分が所有する ★★★
of one's own accord 熟 自発的に ★★★
have one's own way 熟 わがまま勝手に振舞う ★★★
come into one's own 熟 本領を発揮する ★★★
hold one's own 熟 持ちこたえる ★★★
off one's own bat 熟 独力で ★★★
replacement 動 後継者、代理 ★★★
brew 動 （ビールなど）を醸造する ★★★
winery 名 ワイン醸造所 ★★★
distillery 名 蒸留酒製造所 ★★★

解答・解説　answer and explanation

Answer（C）　　　　　　　　　　　　　　　　**Key Point**　最上級

サンライズ・ビール醸造社の新オーナーは、パトリック・ディルジャーに代わって、全米で2番目に大きいビール醸造所の社長になろうとしている。

解法⇒ ＜the ＋序数詞＋最上級＞で「何番目に…」の意味になる。

覚えてトクする語彙

checkup 名 検査、点検 ★★★
medical checkup 名 健康診断 ★★★
dental checkup 名 歯科検査 ★★★
take a rain check 熟 （誘いを受けて都合が悪いとき）また今度にしてもらう ★★★
web 名 くもの巣 ★★★
wed 動 …と結婚する ★★★
surrogate mother 名 代理母（妊娠できない女性の体外受精した卵子を体内で育てて出産する人）★★★

解答・解説　answer and explanation

Answer（B）　　　　　　　　　　　　　　　　**Key Point**　分詞構文

多くの人々が新聞の代用物として、ニュースのウェブサイトを見ることから1日を始める。

解法⇒ コンマ以下は、and many people use them as a kind of surrogate newspaper と書き直すことができる。前半の文と後半の文のつながりが接続詞がなくてもわかるので接続詞を省略し、前半と後半で主語が同じなので主語を省略してある。動詞は、人々が「使っている」ので、using になる。

Chapter1　23

017

Some dietary fats might help prevent Alzheimer's Disease, ------- may increase the risk.

(A) other
(B) others
(C) another
(D) the other

《語彙のヒント》

dietary 形 (栄養から見た) 食べ物の、規定食の ★★★
[dáiətèri]
prevent 動 …をふせぐ ★★★
[privént]
risk 名 危険 ★★★
[rísk]

018

Interested applicants may send their cover letter, curriculum vitae, and transcript of MBA records to the ------- address.

(A) follow
(B) follows
(C) followed
(D) following

《語彙のヒント》

cover letter 名 添え状、添付説明書 ★★★
[kÁvər lètər]
curriculum vitae 名 履歴書、業績書 ★★★
[kəríkjuləm váiti:]
transcript 名 成績証明書 ★★★
[trǽnskript]

第1章 ● パート5 短文穴埋め問題

覚えてトクする語彙

diet 名 ダイエット食、常食 ★★★
Diet 名 (日本などの) 国会 ★★★
prevention 名 防止、予防 ★★★
preventive 形 予防の ★★★
preventive medicine 名 予防医学 ★★★
risk management 名 危機管理
take a [the] risk 熟 あえて危険を冒す ★★★
risky 形 危険な ★★★

解答・解説 answer and explanation

Answer (B) **Key Point** 代名詞

何種類かの食用脂肪はアルツハイマー病の発病を予防するかもしれないが、他のものはアルツハイマー病になる危険性を増やすかもしれない。

解法▶ 普通は fat「脂肪」と不加算名詞として使われることの多い fat が fats と複数形になっていることから、食用脂肪は何種類かあることがわかる。some dietary fats は Alzheimer's Disease「アルツハイマー症（初老期に発生する痴呆症）」発病を予防し、そのほかのものは危険性を増やすのであるから、some dietary fats の複数形と対応させて (B) others「ほかのもの」を選ぶ。

覚えてトクする語彙

application 名 申し込み ★★★
application form 名 申し込み用紙 ★★★
applicable 形 適用できる ★★★
apply 動 申し込む、志願する 《for》 ★★★
applied 形 応用された ★★★
theoretical 形 理論の ★★★
cover story 名 カバーストーリー（雑誌の表紙絵に関した特集記事） ★★★
transcribe 動 …を書き写す、(口述) を文字に起こす ★★★
transcription 名 写し、筆写 ★★★

解答・解説 answer and explanation

Answer (D) **Key Point** 分詞、形容詞

興味のある応募者は、添え状・履歴書・ MBA (Master of Business Administration「経営管理学修士号」) の成績証明書を次の住所にお送りください。

解法▶ 空欄の前後は、前置詞 the と名詞 address なので、形容詞を選ぶ。following は「次の、次にくる」という意味の現在分詞の形容詞である。

019

An applicant must have a successful track record in ------- a business plan and must be a consistent quota achiever.

- (A) achieve
- (B) achieved
- (C) achieving
- (D) to achieve

《語彙のヒント》

track record 名 業績、実績 ★★★
[trǽk rékərd]
consistent 形 首尾一貫した ★★★
[kənsístənt]
quota 名 割り当て量 ★★★
[kwóutə]

020

The Labor Department's report of a moderate increase in inflation helped ------- Wall Street last week.

- (A) soothe
- (B) soothes
- (C) soothing
- (D) being soothed

《語彙のヒント》

moderate 形 まあまあの ★★★
[mádərət]
inflation 名 通貨膨張、インフレ ★★★
[infléiʃən]

覚えてトクする語彙

track 名（行為の）証拠、形跡 動 …の後を追う、（道・進路など）をたどる ★★★
track and filed 名 陸上競技 ★★★
keep track of ~ 熟 …について常に知っている ★★★
achievement test 名 到達度テスト ★★★
consistency 名 一貫性 ★★★
sales quota 名 販売ノルマ ★★★
quote 動 …を引用する ★★★
quotation 名 引用 ★★★
quorum 名（会議成立などに必要な）定足数 ★★★

解答・解説　answer and explanation

Answer (C)　　　　　　　　　　　　　　　　　　　　**Key Point** 動名詞

応募者は、ビジネスの遂行において成功した業績を持ち、一貫したノルマ達成者でなければならない。

解法⇒ 前置詞 in の後なので、achieve「…を達成する」に ing をつけて動名詞にしなければならない。

覚えてトクする語彙

moderately 副 ほどよく ★★★
moderator 名 仲裁者 ★★★
moderation 名 節度 ★★★
inflationary 形 インフレを誘発する ★★★
inflationary spiral 名 悪性インフレ ★★★
inflate 動 …をふくらませる ★★★
soot 名 すす ★★★
sooty 形 すすの、すすだらけの ★★★
chimney sweep 名 煙突掃除人 ★★★

解答・解説　answer and explanation

Answer (A)　　　　　　　　　　　　　　　　　　　　**Key Point** 動詞

労働省の適度なインフレ増加報告は、先週ウォール街を落ち着かせるのに役立った。

解法⇒ help (to) do で「…するのを助ける」であるが、アメリカ英語では、to が省略されることがよくある。soothe は「…を落ち着かせる」という意味である。

021

A key gauge of future ------- activity fell in January, reversing three straight months of gains.

(A) economy
(B) economic
(C) economics
(D) economical

《語彙のヒント》

gauge 名 (評価・判断などの) 基準 ★★★
[géidʒ]
reverse 動 …を逆にする 形 逆の、反対の ★★★
[rivə́ːrs]
gain 名《しばしば複数形で》利益 動 …を (努力の結果) 得る ★★★
[géin]

022

There has been a substantial decrease of ------- 20 percent in airplane fares in the last year.

(A) near
(B) nearly
(C) nearby
(D) nearing

《語彙のヒント》

substantial 形 実質的な ★★★
[səbstǽnʃəl]
fare 名 (バス・鉄道・航空) 運賃 ★★★
[féər]

第1章 ● パート5 短文穴埋め問題

覚えてトクする語彙

keynote 名 (演説・計画などの) 要旨、(政策などの) 基本方針 ★★★
keynote address 名 基調講演 ★★★
key money 名 (家主に払う) 手付金 (= key deposit) ★★★
key in ～ 熟 …を入力する ★★★
economic indicator 名 経済指標 ★★★
economic stimulus measures 名 景気刺激策 ★★★
reversible 形 逆にできる、(衣服などが) 両面仕立ての ★★★
gain ground 熟 前進する、追いつく ★★★

解答・解説　answer and explanation

Answer (B)　　　　　　　　　　　　　　　　**Key Point▶** 品詞、単語

3ヶ月連続の増加とは逆に、将来の経済活動の重要な判断基準は1月に落ちた。

解法▶ 空欄は名詞 activity の直前なので、形容詞が入る。選択肢の中で形容詞は、economic と economical である。economical は「経済的な、節約の」という意味なので、「経済の」という意味の economic を選ぶ。ちなみに economy は「経済」、economics は「経済学」で、こちらもしっかり区別して覚えておこう。

覚えてトクする語彙

substance 名 物質、本質 ★★★
substantially 副 実質上 ★★★
nearby 形 すぐ近くの ★★★
nearsighted 形 近視の ★★★
farewell 形 別れの ★★★
fair 名 見本市 形 公平な ★★★
fair-haired 形 金髪の ★★★
fair-weather 形 まさかのときに役立たない、順境時だけの ★★★
fair to middling 熟 まあまあの ★★★
fair and square 熟 堂々と、公明正大に ★★★

解答・解説　answer and explanation

Answer (B)　　　　　　　　　　　　　　　　**Key Point▶** 副詞

この1年間で、航空運賃は実質20％近くも安くなってきている。

解法▶ 形容詞 near の副詞には、near「近く」と nearly「ほとんど」の2つがあるので、区別して覚えておこう。

023

A contract may be either oral or written; it may be express or implied; it may be formal or simple; it may be entire or -------.

(A) divide
(B) divider
(C) division
(D) divisible

《語彙のヒント》

contract 名 契約 ★★★
[kántrækt]
oral 形 口頭の ★★★
[ɔ́:rəl]
imply 動 …をほのめかす、暗示する ★★★
[implái]

024

We express our great regret for this matter, and have arranged ------- the immediate dispatch of replacements.

(A) at
(B) to
(C) for
(D) from

《語彙のヒント》

regret 名 遺憾 動 …を後悔する ★★★
[rigrét]
dispatch 動 …を急送する ★★★
[dispǽtʃ]
replacement 名 取替品、後任 ★★★
[ripléismənt]

第1章 ● パート5 短文穴埋め問題

覚えてトクする語彙

sign a contract（with ~） 熟 (…と) 契約する ★★★
contraction 名 (筋肉の) 収縮 ★★★
implicit 形 暗黙の ★★★
explicit 形 明白な ★★★
implication 名 ほのめかすこと ★★★
entirely 副 完全に ★★★
divide 動 …を分ける ★★★
division 名 分割、部門 ★★★
dividend 名 (株主への) 配当 (金) ★★★

解答・解説   answer and explanation

Answer（D）   **Key Point** 並列

契約は口頭であったり成文であったり、明示されていたり暗黙的であったり、正式なものであったり簡略化されていたり、全体のものであったり分けられるものであったりする。

解法➡ 接続詞 or の前後は品詞をそろえる。or の前の entire「全体の」は形容詞なので、空欄にも形容詞形である devisible「分けられる」を選ぶ。

覚えてトクする語彙

regretful 形 後悔している ★★★
regrettable 形 残念な ★★★
arrangements 名 手配 ★★★
arranged marriage 名 見合い結婚 ★★★
replace 動 …に取って代わる ★★★
place 動 …を置く、配置する ★★★
placement 名 置くこと、就職斡旋、(学力による) クラス分け ★★★
out of place 熟 その場にそぐわない ★★★
placet 名 賛成 ★★★
placebo 名 気休め薬 ★★★

解答・解説   answer and explanation

Answer（C）   **Key Point** 前置詞

弊社は、この件に関して多大なる遺憾を表明し、ただちに取替品を発送するよう手配いたしました。

解法➡ arrange for ~で、「…を手配する」という意味である。

025

The aircraft engine manufacturer will cut 1,100 jobs as part of a ------- program at three plants.

(A) restructure (B) restructured
(C) restructuring (D) being restructured

《語彙のヒント》

aircraft 名 航空機 ★★★
[éərkræft]

026

This guidebook has sold well over ------- copies and is now in its 8th edition.

(A) a million half (B) half a million
(C) million half (D) million a half

《語彙のヒント》

copy 名 写し、(同時に印刷された本・雑誌などの) 1 部 動 …を写す、まねる ★★★
[kápi]
edition 名 版 ★★★
[idíʃən]

第1章 ● パート5 短文穴埋め問題

覚えてトクする語彙

air cargo 名 空輸貨物 ★★★
airfreight 名 貨物空輸便（業） ★★★
airfare 名 航空運賃 ★★★
air turbulence 名 乱気流 ★★★
Air Force 名 米国空軍 ★★★
Air Force One 名 エアフォースワン（米大統領専用機） ★★★
air conditioner 名 クーラー ★★★
airhead 名 ばか、からっぽ頭 ★★★
airtight 形 （論理などが）すきのない ★★★
airlift 動 …を空輸する ★★★

解答・解説　answer and explanation

Answer （C）　**Key Point** 品詞

その航空機エンジン製造業者は、事業再編成プログラムの一部として、3つの工場で1100の仕事をカットした。

解法→ restructuring は「事業の再構築、構造改革」という意味である。名詞だが、program の前に置かれて形容詞の働きをしている。日本語の「リストラ」は「人員削減」のイメージが強いが、「人員削減」は英語では downsizing という。

覚えてトクする語彙

guidance 名 （…についての）指導、案内 ★★★
guideline 名 指針 ★★★
over and above 熟 その上 ★★★
over the top 熟 大げさに ★★★
over one's dead body 熟 絶対に…させない ★★★
over and over again 熟 繰り返し、何度も何度も ★★★
hand over fist 熟 どんどん、すばやく ★★★
tide over ～ 熟 …を乗り切る、切り抜ける ★★★
hold over ～ 熟 …を延期する ★★★
copier 名 複写機、コピー機（= photocopier） ★★★

解答・解説　answer and explanation

Answer （B）　**Key Point** 形容詞、名詞

このガイドブックはかるく50万部以上売れていて、現在第8版を数えている。

解法→ 時間・数量の単位をいうとき、half a ～と a half ～の2つの形がある。half a million の half は、元来は形容詞であるが、half of a million の of が省略された名詞とみなすこともできる。

027

Food retailing and packaging in this nation's supermarkets will soon ------- drastic changes.

(A) underdo (B) undergo
(C) underrun (D) underwrite

《語彙のヒント》

retail 動 …を小売する　名 小売り　形 小売りの　★★★
[ríːteil]
package 動 …を包装する　名 荷物　形 ひとまとめの　★★★
[pækidʒ]
drastic 形 劇的な、抜本的な　★★★
[drǽstik]

028

Recent research shows that Americans work the longest hours of all workers in ------- advanced countries.

(A) industrious (B) industrial
(C) industriously (D) industrially

《語彙のヒント》

research 名 調査、研究　動 研究する《into, on》　★★★
[risə́ːrtʃ]
advanced 形 前進した、進歩した　★★★
[ædvǽnst]

第1章 ● パート5 短文穴埋め問題

覚えてトクする語彙

retailer 名 小売商人 ★★★
package tour 名 (旅行社が企画する) パック旅行 ★★★
underwriter 名 保険業者、証券引受人 ★★★
underlie 動 …の下に横たわる ★★★
underscore 動 …に下線を引く ★★★
underpin 動 …を確証する ★★★
undertake 動 …を引き受ける ★★★
dramatic 形 演劇の、劇的な ★★★

解答・解説 answer and explanation

Answer (B)　　　　　　　　　　　　　　　　　　　　　***Key Point*** 単語

この国のスーパーマーケットの食品の小売りと包装は、間もなく劇的な変化を経験するだろう。

解法➡ 空欄の後に drastic changes「劇的な変化」が来ているので、文意から判断して (B) undergo「…を経験する」が適切である。ちなみに、(A) underdo は「…をふつう以下にする」、(C) underrun は「…の下を走る」、(D) underwrite は「…に署名する」という意味である。

覚えてトクする語彙

researcher 名 研究者 ★★★
research and development 名 研究開発 (= R & D) ★★★
industrial waste water 名 工場廃水 ★★★
industrialist 名 産業経営者 ★★★
industrialism 名 産業主義 ★★★
industrialize 動 …を産業化する、工業化する ★★★
developing country 名 発展途上国 ★★★
advance 動 …を前進させる 名 前進、株価上昇 ★★★
in advance 熟 前もって、あらかじめ ★★★
advancement 名 昇進 ★★★

解答・解説 answer and explanation

Answer (D)　　　　　　　　　　　　　　　　　　　　***Key Point*** 単語、副詞

最近の調査によると、アメリカ人は、先進工業国の中で一番長い時間働いているという。

解法➡ (A) industrious「勤勉な」と (B) industrial「工業の」の意味をしっかり区別しよう。空欄は、形容詞 advanced を修飾するので、副詞 (D) industrially「工業的に」を選ぶ。なお、advanced industrial country「先進工業国」の場合は、industrial は名詞 country を修飾するので、形容詞 industrial となる。

029

Almost two-thirds of homes in Alaska have a computer, but only one quarter of homes in Mississippi -------.

(A) is
(B) are
(C) do
(D) does

《語彙のヒント》

quarter 图 4分の1、(米国・カナダの) 25セント硬貨、四半期 ★★★
[kwɔ́ːrtər]

030

Farmers could grow a record corn crop this year ------- the weather is better than last year.

(A) if
(B) not
(C) without
(D) whether

《語彙のヒント》

farmer 图 農業経営者 ★★★
[fáːrmər]
record 图 記録 ★★★
[rékərd]
crop 图 作物、収穫高 ★★★
[krάp]

覚えてトクする語彙

home economics 名 家政学、家庭科 ★★★
homemade 形 自家製の ★★★
homemaker 名 主婦 ★★★
quartet 名 4人組 ★★★
quarterly 形 年4回の、季ごとの ★★★
dime 名 (米国・カナダの) 10セント硬貨 ★★★
a dime a dozen 熟 ありふれた、安っぽい ★★★
nickel 名 (米・カナダの) 5セント硬貨 ★★★
penny 名 (米・カナダの) 1セント硬貨 ★★★

解答・解説 answer and explanation

Answer (C)　　　　　　　　　　　　　　**Key Point** 代動詞

アラスカの家庭のほぼ3分の2はコンピュータを持っているが、ミシシッピでは4分の1しか持っていない。

解法⇒ 接続詞 but 以下は、only one quarter of homes in Mississippi have a computer. なので、have a computer が前半の繰り返しになるため、代動詞 do で置き換える。

覚えてトクする語彙

farm 名 農場 ★★★
farming 名 農業、飼育、養殖 ★★★
farmfresh vegetables 名 産地直送野菜 ★★★
grownup 名 成人、大人 (adult よりもくだけた語) ★★★
record holder 名 記録保持者 ★★★
off the record 熟 秘密に、非公開に ★★★
crop circle 名 ミステリーサークル (英国南部に多い畑の小麦などが円形になぎ倒された跡) ★★★
crop up 熟 突然生じる ★★★

解答・解説 answer and explanation

Answer (A)　　　　　　　　　　　　　　**Key Point** 接続詞

もし天気が昨年よりよければ、農業従事者は今年、記録的なとうもろこしの収穫高を期待できるだろう。

解法⇒ 前半に主語 (farmers)・動詞 (could grow) がそろっており、後半も主語 (the weather)・動詞 (is) がそろっているので、文と文をつなげる接続詞を選ぶ。文脈から if が正解である。

031

A building at the Centers for Disease Control was evacuated briefly after a false fire -------.

(A) alarm
(B) alarms
(C) alarmed
(D) alarming

《語彙のヒント》

evacuate 動 …を立ち退かせる、避難させる、からにする ★★★
[ivǽkjuèit]
briefly 副 ちょっとの間、簡潔に ★★★
[brí:fli]
false 形 誤った ★★★
[fɔ́:ls]

032

Our hotel combines the spirit and culture of the islands ------- the luxury and amenities of a world class resort.

(A) on
(B) for
(C) with
(D) about

《語彙のヒント》

combine 動 …を結合して一体にする《with》 ★★★
[kəmbáin]
luxury 名 ぜいたく ★★★
[lʌ́kʃəri]
amenity 名 備品、設備 ★★★
[əménəti]

覚えてトクする語彙

evacuation 名 避難 ★★★
brief 形 短時間の、(文体・表現が) 簡潔な 動 …に報告する 名 摘要 (書) ★★★
briefing 名 簡単な報告、説明会 ★★★
briefcase 名 ブリーフケース、書類かばん ★★★
in brief 熟 要するに ★★★
false alarm 名 (消防署への) 誤った火災通報 ★★★
false praise 名 お世辞 (= flattery) ★★★
alarm clock 名 目覚まし時計 ★★★
burglar alarm 名 盗難予防用自動警報機 ★★★
alarming 形 (悪いことの増加が) 深刻な ★★★

解答・解説 answer and explanation

Answer (A) **Key Point** 単語

誤った火災警報の後、少しの間、疾病対策センターの建物には人がいなくなった。

解法▶ 名詞 fire alarm「火災警報」の前に、形容詞の false が置かれて「誤った火災警報」の意味となる。

覚えてトクする語彙

combination 名 結合 ★★★
combined pollution 名 複合汚染 ★★★
combo 名 (特にファーストフードの店で) 料理の組み合わせ ★★★
comb 動 …をくまなく捜す ★★★
spiritual 形 精神の ★★★
spiritual song 名 聖歌、賛美歌 ★★★
spirituality 名 精神的であること ★★★
luxurious 形 ぜいたくな ★★★
luscious 形 おいしい、甘美な ★★★
as a last resort 熟 最後の手段として ★★★

解答・解説 answer and explanation

Answer (C) **Key Point** 前置詞、熟語

私どものホテルは島の精神・文化と世界一流のリゾート設備・ぜいたくさを併せ持っています。

解法▶ combine A with B で「A を B と組み合わせる」の意味を表す重要表現である。

033

Unlicensed and drunken drivers continue to get behind ------- and have accidents despite tougher laws.

(A) wheel
(B) wheels
(C) a wheel
(D) the wheel

《語彙のヒント》

unlicensed 形 無免許の ★★★
[ʌ̀nláisənst]
continue 動 …を続ける《to *do*, *doing*》 ★★★
[kəntínjuː]
tough 形 きびしい ★★★
[tʌ́f]

034

They plan ------- an Indian communications satellite into orbit around the end of March.

(A) send
(B) sent
(C) sending
(D) to send

《語彙のヒント》

communications satellite 名 通信衛星 ★★★
[kəmjùːnəkéiʃənz sǽtəlàit]
orbit 名 軌道 ★★★
[ɔ́ːrbit]

第1章 ● パート5 短文穴埋め問題

覚えてトクする語彙

license 图 免許、許可 ★★★
license plate 图 車のナンバープレート ★★★
driver's license 图 車の免許 ★★★
licensing fees 图 ライセンス使用料 ★★★
continual 形 絶え間のない、連続的な ★★★
continuous 形 切れずにつながった ★★★
continuation 图 続くこと、続き ★★★
continuity 图 連続、継続性 ★★★
continuum 图 連続体 ★★★
discontinue 動 …をやめる《doing》 ★★★

解答・解説

Answer (D) **Key Point** 熟語

よりきびしい法律にもかかわらず、無免許で飲酒しているドライバーが運転し、事故を起こし続けている。

解法 get behind the wheel で「車を運転する」という熟語である。

覚えてトクする語彙

communications 图 通信機関、報道機関 ★★★
communication 图 意思伝達 ★★★
communicate 動 …を伝える、知らせる ★★★
communication gap 图 相互理解の欠如 ★★★
mass communication 图 マスコミ、大衆伝達 ★★★
satellite 图 人工衛星、衛星 ★★★
satellite television 图 衛星テレビ ★★★
satellite broadcasting 图 衛星放送 ★★★
orbital 形 軌道の ★★★

解答・解説

Answer (D) **Key Point** 不定詞

3月の終わりごろ、インドの通信衛星を軌道に乗せる予定だ。

解法 動詞 plan は、目的語に動名詞ではなく to 不定詞をとる。目的語に to 不定詞をとる動詞は他に、agree「同意する」、decide「決定する」、expect「期待する」、hope「望む」、intend「意図する」、pretend「ふりをする」、promise「約束する」、refuse「拒絶する」、resolve「決心する」、swear「誓う」、wish「望む」などがあるので、あわせて確認しておこう。

035

Our representatives in London have asked for a ------- for 20 units of your new product model PF-200.

(A) quote
(B) quoted
(C) quoting
(D) quotation

《語彙のヒント》

representative 名 代表者、代理人 ★★★
[rèprizéntətiv]
unit 名 (機械・装備の) 1セット・1個、(計量の) 単位 ★★★
[júːnit]

036

In early America, tipping was felt ------- a European practice, one that was corrupt, illegal and downright undemocratic.

(A) be
(B) being
(C) to be
(D) to being

《語彙のヒント》

tip 動 チップをやる 名 チップ、心づけ ★★★
[típ]
corrupt 形 不正な、堕落した 動 堕落する、買収される ★★★
[kərápt]
downright 副 完全に、まぎれもなく 形 まったくの ★★★
[dáunràit]

42 Chapter1

第1章 ● パート5 短文穴埋め問題

覚えてトクする語彙

represent 動 …を表す、代表する ★★★
representation 名 代表、表現 ★★★
diplomatic representative 名 外交官 ★★★
sales representative 名 セールスマン ★★★
Representative 名 米国下院議員（= Congressman） ★★★
quotable 形 引用できる、引用する価値がある ★★★
quota 名 割り当て ★★★
unit cost 名 単価 ★★★
unit price 名 セット料金 ★★★

解答・解説 answer and explanation

Answer (D) **Key Point▶** 品詞

弊社のロンドン駐在員が、御社の新製品PF-200型20台の値段の見積もりをたずねてきました。

解法▶ 空欄は、不定冠詞aの後であり、意味を考えて名詞 quotation「値段の見積もり」が正解。なお、quoteには「値段をつける、…を引用する」という意味がある。

覚えてトクする語彙

tip-off 名 秘密情報 ★★★
tip off 熟 …に密告する、内報する ★★★
corruption 名 堕落 ★★★
downplay 動 …を軽視する ★★★
downsize 動 …を削減する、縮小する ★★★
downsized 形 小型化した ★★★
down payment 名 頭金 ★★★
downturn 名 下落、下降 ★★★
downpour 名 どしゃ降り ★★★

解答・解説 answer and explanation

Answer (C) **Key Point▶** 不定詞

初期のアメリカでは、チップは、腐敗し、非合法的で、きわめて非民主主義的なヨーロッパの慣習だと考えられていた。

解法▶ 問題文は <feel + 目的語 + to be（+ 補語）> が受動態になっている。feel の他、think、guess、report、believe、know などが <S + V + O + to be ～> の構文で用いられる。

037

The "Ten Commandments" are quoted on many occasions: in presidential speeches, and in book titles, to name -------.

(A) few
(B) little
(C) a few
(D) a little

《語彙のヒント》

Ten Commandments 名 十戒（神が Sinai 山において Moses を通してイスラエル人に与えた 10 項目の戒め） ★★★
[tén kəmǽndmənts]
occasion 名 （特定の）時、場合 ★★★
[əkéiʒən]
presidential 形 大統領の ★★★
[prèzədénʃəl]

038

When a corporation, partnership, or sole proprietorship is dissolved or sold, legal counsel is -------.

(A) essence
(B) essential
(C) essentially
(D) essentiality

《語彙のヒント》

proprietorship 名 所有者団体、所有権 ★★★
[prəpráiətərʃip]
dissolve 動 （組織を）解散する、（関係を）解消する、（契約など）を解除する ★★★
[dizálv]
counsel 名 相談、協議 ★★★
[káunsəl]

第1章 ● パート5 短文穴埋め問題

覚えてトクする語彙

commandment 名 命令、戒律 ★★★
command 動 …を命じる ★★★
commandant 名 司令官、指揮官 ★★★
commandeer 動 …を軍務に徴収する、勝手に取り上げる ★★★
commander 名 命令者、指揮者 ★★★
occasional 形 時折の ★★★
occasionally 副 ときどき ★★★
rise to the occasion 熟 難局にうまく対処する ★★★
presidential election 名 米大統領選挙 ★★★
presidential primary 名 (各政党の) 米大統領予備選挙 ★★★

解答・解説

Answer (C) **Key Point** 熟語

「十戒」は、多くの機会に引用され、2～3例を挙げれば、大統領の演説、本の題名などがある。

解法➡ to name a few で「少数の名［例］を挙げれば」という熟語である。

覚えてトクする語彙

corporation tax 名 法人税 ★★★
sole representative 名 総代理人 ★★★
solely 副 単独で、単に ★★★
proprietor 名 (企業・ホテル・商店などの) 所有者、経営者 ★★★
proprietary 形 製造販売の独占権を持つ、専売特許の ★★★
proprietary name 名 登録名、商標名 ★★★
proprietary company 名 親会社、持ち株会社 ★★★
dissolution 名 解消、解除 ★★★
juridical counselor 名 法律顧問 ★★★

解答・解説

Answer (B) **Key Point** 品詞

有限会社、合名会社、独占所有者組織が解散されたり売却されたときには、法的な協議が不可欠となる。

解法➡ 空欄は legal counsel is の後だから、形容詞 essential が入る。

Chapter1 45

039

The item under your inquiry has just been sold out, and we are not ------- a position to quote on it.

(A) at
(B) in
(C) for
(D) toward

《語彙のヒント》

item 名 品目 ★★★
[áitəm]
sell out ~ 動 …を売り切る ★★★
[sél áut]
quote 動 …の値を見積もる、の相場をつける ★★★
[kwóut]

040

Japanese paychecks have been dwindling, with even major automakers ------- pay raises this year.

(A) holding
(B) beholding
(C) upholding
(D) withholding

《語彙のヒント》

paycheck 名 給料 ★★★
[péitʃèk]
dwindle 動 …をだんだん小さくする ★★★
[dwíndl]

第1章 ● パート5 短文穴埋め問題

覚えてトクする語彙

itemize 動 …を項目別に述べる、記入する、…の明細を示す ★★★
sell ~ short 熟 …をあなどる、安売りする ★★★
sell like hot cakes 熟 飛ぶように売れる ★★★
sell *a person* down the river 熟 …を裏切る、欺く ★★★
posit 動 …を事実と仮定する ★★★
be in position 熟 正しい位置にある ★★★
be out of position 熟 おかしな位置にある ★★★
quotation 名 （商品・証券などの）相場付け、時価の見積もり、相場 ★★★

解答・解説 answer and explanation

Answer (B)　　　　　　　　　　　　　　　　**Key Point** 前置詞、熟語
お問い合わせの商品は売り切れで、私どもはその値段をつけることができません。
解法➡ be in a position to *do* で、「立場にある」という意味である。その否定形としては、be in no position to *do* や be not in a position to *do* などがよく用いられる。

覚えてトクする語彙

payment 名 納入金、支払金 ★★★
payroll 名 給料支払い名簿、従業員総数 ★★★
payday 名 給料日 ★★★
payback 名 払い戻し、報復 ★★★
withstand 動 …に持ちこたえる、抵抗する ★★★
withdraw 動 …を引き出す ★★★
belittle 動 …を過小評価する ★★★
bewitch 動 （人）を魅了する ★★★
upstage 動 （社会的・職業的地位において）…をしのぐ ★★★

解答・解説 answer and explanation

Answer (D)　　　　　　　　　　　　　　　　**Key Point** 単語
日本人の給料は、大手自動車メーカーでさえ今年賃上げを控えているほどで、だんだん減ってきた。
解法➡ 空欄に適切な現在分詞を入れる問題である。文脈から「大手自動車メーカーでさえ賃上げを…しており」の意味と解釈できるので、withhold「…を差し控える、見合わせる」の現在分詞形である (D) を選ぶ。(B) behold は「…を注視する」、(C) uphold は「…を持ち上げる」の意味である。

041

It will be cloudy with a chance of rain ------- with snow this evening.

(A) mix (B) mixed
(C) mixing (D) mixture

《語彙のヒント》

cloudy 形 曇った ★★★
[kláudi]

042

The American Cancer Society is about to start a drive to encourage people ------- weight and get more active.

(A) lose (B) lost
(C) losing (D) to lose

《語彙のヒント》

cancer 名 がん ★★★
[kǽnsər]
drive 名 (組織的) 運動 ★★★
[dráiv]

第1章 ● パート5 短文穴埋め問題

覚えてトクする語彙

cloudless 形 晴れ渡った ★★★
have *one's* head in the clouds 熟 空想にふけっている ★★★
be on cloud nine 熟 この上なく幸せである ★★★
snowy 形 雪の多い ★★★
flurry 名 突風 ★★★
blizzard 名 猛吹雪 ★★★
mix A up with B 熟 AをBと混同する ★★★
mixture 名 混合物 ★★★
mixer 名 交際上手な人 ★★★
mix-up 名 混乱 ★★★

解答・解説

Answer (B) **Key Point ▸** 過去分詞

今晩は、曇って、みぞれが降る可能性がある。

解法 ➡ 空欄の前の名詞 rain を修飾するためには、現在分詞 mixing か過去分詞 mixed かどちらかが正解の候補となる。「雨が混ぜている」のではなく、「雨が混ぜられている」ので、過去分詞 mixed を選ぶ。

覚えてトクする語彙

cancerous 形 がんの、手に負えない ★★★
gastric cancer 名 胃がん ★★★
breast cancer 名 乳がん ★★★
the lost and found 名 遺失物取扱所 ★★★
lose face 熟 評判を落とす ★★★
lose *one's* temper 熟 かっとなる ★★★
lose no time (**in**) **doing** 熟 すぐ…する ★★★
lose *one's* shirt 熟 大損をする、無一文になる ★★★
lose sleep over [**about**] ~ 熟 《通常否定文で》…を大変心配する ★★★

解答・解説

Answer (D) **Key Point ▸** 不定詞

アメリカがん協会は、体重を減らし、もっと活動的になることを奨励する運動を始めるところだ。

解法 ➡ 動詞 encourage は <encourage +目的語+ to *do*> で「人が…するように奨励する、励ます」の意味である。よって、空欄には to 不定詞を入れる。

043

Shaw Energy Inc. is examining the ways to ------- its 77 percent stake in the OPP security alarm company.

(A) diverge (B) divert
(C) divest   (D) divulge

《語彙のヒント》

Inc. 名 株式会社（= incorporated） ★★★
[íŋk]
stake 名 出資額、出資額相当の株 ★★★
[stéik]
security 名 安全、防衛 ★★★
[sikjúərəti]

044

Credit cards can be used almost anywhere, ------- of restaurants, supermarkets, and even little mom-and-pop stores.

(A) include   (B) included
(C) including (D) inclusive

《語彙のヒント》

credit 名 （客への）信用 ★★★
[krédit]
mom-and-pop 形 夫婦（家族）経営の、零細な ★★★
[mámənpáp]

第1章 ● パート5 短文穴埋め問題

覚えてトクする語彙

divergence 名 分岐、(意見などの) 相違 ★★★
divergent 形 (一点から) 分かれ出る、(意見などが) 相違する ★★★
diversion 名 気晴らし ★★★
divulgence 名 暴露 ★★★
secure 形 安全な ★★★
security guard 名 警備員 ★★★
security screening 名 手荷物検査 ★★★
Security Council 名 《the ~》(国連の) 安全保障理事会 ★★★
U.S.-Japan Security Treaty 名 《the ~》日米安全保障条約 ★★★

解答・解説

Answer (C) **Key Point** 単語

ショー・エネルギー社は、OPP防犯警報器会社に出資した株式の77％を売却する方法を吟味している。

解法 「出資した株式の77％を…する」という文脈から、「(持ち株・子会社など) を売却する」という意味の (C) divest が適切である。(A) diverge は「(一点から) 分かれ出る」、(B) divert は「…を迂回させる、…の進路を変える」(D) divulge は「(私事・秘密) を漏らす」という意味である。

覚えてトクする語彙

creditable 形 (人の) 名誉となる ★★★
creditability 名 名誉 ★★★
credible 形 (人・供述が) 信じられる ★★★
credibility 名 信用できること ★★★
creditor 名 債権者 ★★★
debtor 名 債務者 ★★★
credit card 名 クレジットカード ★★★
credit union 名 信用組合 ★★★
credit line 名 (銀行の) 貸出限度額 ★★★
give *a person* credit for ~ 熟 …を人の手柄とする ★★★

解答・解説

Answer (D) **Key Point** 熟語

クレジットカードは、レストランやスーパーマーケット、小さな自営業店をも含む、あらゆる場所で使える。

解法 空欄の後に of があるので、inclusive of ~「…を含めて」を選ぶ。inclusive of ~ = including なので、of がなければ including「…を含む」が入る。

045

A plan to help ------- the airline out of bankruptcy would risk retirement security for nearly 50 million people in the country.

(A) bar (B) bail
(C) barb (D) barter

《語彙のヒント》

bankruptcy 名 破産 ★★★
[bǽŋkrʌptsi]
risk 動 …を危険にさらす ★★★
[rísk]
retirement 名 退職 ★★★
[ritáiərmənt]

046

They are now developing new technology to help companies control their ------- documents.

(A) intern (B) internal
(C) internality (D) internalize

《語彙のヒント》

document 名 (通常複数形で) 書類 ★★★
[dákjumənt]

第1章 ● パート5 短文穴埋め問題

覚えてトクする語彙

bankrupt 形 破産した 動 …を破産させる ★★★
go [into] bankruptcy 熟 破産する ★★★
retired 形 退職した、引退した ★★★
retiring 形 内気な、控えめな ★★★
retiree 名 退職者 ★★★
retirement pay 名 退職金 ★★★
retirement benefits 名 退職手当 ★★★
voluntary [early] retirement 名 （定年前の）希望退職、早期退職 ★★★

解答・解説

Answer (B) **Key Point** 単語

その航空会社を破産から救済する計画は、ほぼ5000万人の国民の退職後の保障を危険にさらすことになるだろう。

解法 「その航空会社を破産から…するのを助ける計画」という文脈から、bail「…を救済する」が適切である。(A) bar は「…をふさぐ、禁じる」、(C) barb は「（釣り針・やじりなどに）かかりをつける」、(D) barter《for》は「…を物々交換する」という意味である。

覚えてトクする語彙

internal audit 名 内部監査 ★★★
internal medicine 名 内科 ★★★
internal organs 名 内臓 ★★★
external 名 外部の ★★★
external pressure 名 外圧 ★★★
external medicine 名 外用薬 ★★★
externality 名 外面性 ★★★
externalize 動 …を外面化する ★★★
externalization 名 具体化 ★★★

解答・解説

Answer (B) **Key Point** 品詞

彼らは、会社が内部文書を管理するのを助けることのできる新しい技術を開発中である。

解法 空欄は、代名詞の所有格 their と名詞 documents「書類」の間であるから、名詞を修飾する形容詞 (B) internal「内部の」が入る。(A) intern は「見習い、実習生」、(C) internality は「内面性」、(D) internalize は「…を内面化する」という意味である。

047

From banking to real estate and state taxes, this special report ------- you how your finances can be affected.

(A) says (B) tells
(C) says to (D) tells to

《語彙のヒント》

banking 名 銀行取引 ★★★
[bǽŋkiŋ]
real estate 名 不動産 ★★★
[ríːəl istèit]
finance 名 財政、資本 ★★★
[finǽns]

048

City Manager Marcia Conner is scheduled to attend ------- executive training session in St. Paul this spring.

(A) five-day (B) five-days
(C) a five-day (D) a five-days

《語彙のヒント》

manager 名 支配人、管理人 ★★★
[mǽnidʒər]
attend 動 …に出席する ★★★
[əténd]
executive 名 経営幹部、重役 ★★★
[igzékjutiv]

第1章 ● パート5 短文穴埋め問題

覚えてトクする語彙

bank [動] 預金する ★★★
banker [名] 銀行業者 ★★★
bankroll [動] （資金）を提供する ★★★
bank [count] on ~ [熟] …を当てにする、頼る ★★★
estate [名] 財産 ★★★
personal estate [名] 動産 ★★★
estate tax [名] 相続税 ★★★
financier [名] 出資者 ★★★
public finance [名] 国家財政 ★★★
finance company [名] （企業相手の）金融会社 ★★★

解答・解説 answer and explanation

Answer （B） **Key Point・** 動詞

銀行取引から不動産や州税まで、この特別報告書には、個人財政がどのように影響を受けるかが書かれている。

解法→ 空欄の後に、間接目的語 you と、直接目的語 how 節の2つの目的語があるので、目的語を2つ取ることができる動詞 tell が正解である。

覚えてトクする語彙

manage [動] …を管理する ★★★
management [名] 操作、管理 ★★★
manageable [形] 操作しやすい ★★★
crisis management [名] 危機管理 ★★★
executive committee [名] 実行委員会 ★★★
executive board [名] 理事会 ★★★
Chief Executive Officer [名] 最高経営責任者（= CEO） ★★★
execute [動] （職務など）を実行する、…を処刑する ★★★
execution [名] 遂行、執行、死刑執行 ★★★
study session [名] 勉強会 ★★★

解答・解説 answer and explanation

Answer （C） **Key Point・** 形容詞

市の主任マーシャ・コナーは、この春セント・ポールで行われる5日間の行政官養成会議に出席する予定だ。

解法→ a three-year old girl のように数字が形容詞の一部として組み込まれるとき、複数形のsは必要なくなる。また、session「会議・議会などの開会」は可算名詞であるので、不定冠詞 a が必要である。

Chapter1 ■■■ 55

049

It is ------- that multi-function "smart cards" will become common by the year 2010.

(A) estimate
(B) estimated
(C) estimating
(D) estimation

《語彙のヒント》

multi-function 形 多機能の ★★★
[mʌ́ltifʌ́ŋkʃən]
smart card 名 スマートカード（情報を記憶するカード） ★★★
[smáːrt kàːrd]

050

With the real estate industry ------- new headlines everyday, everyone wants to know what we can expect for the future.

(A) make
(B) made
(C) making
(D) being made

《語彙のヒント》

headline 名 《通常複数形で》(新聞の) 大見出し ★★★
[hédlàin]

第1章 ● パート5 短文穴埋め問題

覚えてトクする語彙

estimative 形 評価できる ★★★
estimator 名 見積もり人 ★★★
multi-factorial 形 さまざまな原因によって起こる ★★★
multi-national 形 多国籍の ★★★
multi-purpose 形 多用途の ★★★
multilateral 形 多面的な、多数国の ★★★
multilingual 形 多言語を話せる ★★★
multiple 形 多数からなる ★★★
multiple-choice 形 多項式選択の ★★★
smart 形 賢い ★★★

解答・解説

Answer (B)　　　　　　　　　　　　　　**Key Point** 動詞、受動態

2010年までに、多機能のスマートカードが一般的になると見込まれている。

解法 ▶ 空欄は It is と that の間であるので、that 以下のことが「見込まれている」と、estimate「…であると見積もる、…と察する」の受動態である (B) estimated が適切である。ちなみに (D) estimation は「判断」という意味である。

覚えてトクする語彙

headquarters 名 本部、本社 ★★★
headlong 副 軽率に ★★★
make headway 熟 前進する、進歩する ★★★
make the grade 熟 成功する、うまくいく ★★★
make time 熟 急ぐ、早く進む ★★★
make good 熟 成功する、うまくいく ★★★
make sense 熟 意味をなす、道理にかなっている ★★★
make waves 熟 波風を立てる ★★★
make a splash 熟 大評判をとる、あっと言わせる ★★★

解答・解説

Answer (C)　　　　　　　　　　　　　　**Key Point** 現在分詞

不動産業は毎日、新聞の見出しを飾っているので、将来何が期待できるのか皆が知りたがっている。

解法 ▶ make (the) headlines で「見出しになる、報道される」という熟語であり、「新しい見出しになっている」のだから、現在分詞の (C) making を選ぶ。文頭の with は付帯状況を表す。

051

Japan ranks around 22nd worldwide in per ------- consumption of beer.

(A) capita (B) capital
(C) capitol (D) capitate

《語彙のヒント》

rank 動 順位を占める ★★★
[rǽŋk]

052

Excellent social skills and negotiation skills are indispensable ------- a successful sales representative.

(A) be (B) being
(C) to been (D) to being

《語彙のヒント》

excellent 形 すばらしい、優秀な ★★★
[éksələnt]
negotiation 名 交渉 ★★★
[nigòuʃiéiʃən]
indispensable 形 欠くことのできない ★★★
[ìndispénsəbl]

第1章 ● パート5 短文穴埋め問題

覚えてトクする語彙

ranking 名 順位、ランキング ★★★
rank and file 名 大衆、一般人 ★★★
per 前 …につき、ごとに ★★★
per annum 副 1年ごとに ★★★
per diem 副 1日につき ★★★
capitalize 動 …を大文字で書く、…に出資する ★★★
capitalize on ～ 熟 …でもうける、利用する ★★★
capital assets 名 固定資産 ★★★
capital gains 名 （株式などの）資産売却所得 ★★★
capital punishment 名 死刑、極刑 ★★★

■解答・解説　answer and explanation

Answer (A)　*Key Point* ▸ 熟語

日本は世界で、ビールの消費量1人当たり22位である。

解法➡ per capita で「1人当たりの」という意味である。(A) capital は「資本（金）」、(C) capitol は「米国の州議会議事堂」、(D) capitate は「（植物学で）頭上の」という意味である。

覚えてトクする語彙

excellence 名 優秀 ★★★
excel 動 …にまさる ★★★
sociable 形 社交好きな ★★★
socialize 動 （人）を社交的にする ★★★
socialism 名 社会主義 ★★★
social security 名 社会保障（制度） ★★★
social studies 名 （単数扱いで）社会科 ★★★
negotiate 動 交渉する ★★★
negotiable 形 交渉の余地がある ★★★
negotiator 名 交渉者 ★★★

■解答・解説　answer and explanation

Answer (D)　*Key Point* ▸ 熟語、動名詞

セールスマンとして成功するには、優秀な社交・交渉技能が不可欠である。

解法➡ indispensable to ～「…にとって不可欠な」の to は、不定詞でなく前置詞である。to の代わりに for を用いることもできる。問題文の空欄に入る (D) to being の being は動名詞である。

053

It is against the law to drive a motor vehicle ------- streets and highways without a valid driver license.

(A) at (B) on
(C) for (D) above

《語彙のヒント》

motor vehicle 名 自動車 ★★★
[móutər vìːikl]
valid 形 正当な、有効な ★★★
[vǽlid]

054

Technology is constantly changing and ------- the telecommunications industry.

(A) is (B) is so
(C) so is (D) so that is

《語彙のヒント》

constantly 副 絶え間なく ★★★
[kánstəntli]
telecommunications 名 電気通信 ★★★
[tèləkəmjunəkéiʃənz]

覚えてトクする語彙

against the clock [熟] せかされて ★★★
go against the [*one's*] grain with ~ [熟] …の性に合わない ★★★
for or against ~ [熟] …に賛成か反対か ★★★
lean against ~ [熟] …にもたれる ★★★
rebel against ~ [熟] …に背く、反発する ★★★
be dead set against ~ [熟] …に猛反対である ★★★
beat *one's* head against a wall [熟] 無理な事をする ★★★
have two strikes against one [熟] 不利な立場に置かれている ★★★
validity [名] 妥当(性) ★★★

解答・解説 answer and explanation

Answer (B)   ***Key Point*** 前置詞
法的に有効な運転免許証を持たずに自動車を運転することは、違法である。
解法 ➡ 「道路上で」というときは、アメリカ英語では on を用い、イギリス英語では in を用いる。

覚えてトクする語彙

constant [形] 不変の ★★★
telecommunicate [動] (データ・声・映像など)を遠距離通信で送る ★★★
telecommute [動] 在宅勤務する ★★★
telecommuting [名] (コンピュータ通信による)在宅勤務 ★★★
teleconference [名] (テレビ電話などによる)遠隔地間会議 ★★★
telegram [名] 電報 ★★★
telegraph [名] (通信手段としての)電信 ★★★
teleshopping [名] テレビショッピング ★★★
telemarketing [名] 電話による商品販売 ★★★
televise [動] …をテレビで放送する ★★★

解答・解説 answer and explanation

Answer (C)   ***Key Point*** 倒置
科学技術は絶え間なく変化し、電気通信産業もしかりである。
解法 ➡ 肯定文に続いて、「…もまた~である」というときには、<and + so + V + S> という形になり、倒置が起こる。

055

Major airlines are now offering a wider ------- of cheap fares aimed at corporate fliers.

　　(A) ally　　　　　　(B) allay
　　(C) alley　　　　　 (D) array

《語彙のヒント》

fare 名 運賃 ★★★
[féər]
aim 動 ねらう《at》 ★★★
[éim]
flier 名 航空機の旅客 ★★★
[fláiər]

056

Statistics say that single working people now comprise of ------- all U.S. households.

　　(A) one-third　　　　(B) one-three
　　(C) one-thirds　　　 (D) one-threes

《語彙のヒント》

statistics 名 統計（複数扱い）、統計学（単数扱い） ★★★
[stətístiks]
comprise 動 構成する《of》 ★★★
[kəmpráiz]
household 名 世帯、家庭 ★★★
[háushòuld]

第1章 ● パート5 短文穴埋め問題

覚えてトクする語彙

aimless 形 目的の無い ★★★
fly 動 飛ぶ ★★★
fly off the handle 熟 かっとなる《at》 ★★★
fly the coop 熟 ずらかる、脱走する ★★★
fry 動 …を油で揚げる ★★★

解答・解説　answer and explanation

Answer (D)　　　　　　　　　　　　　　　　　　　**Key Point** 単語

大手航空会社は今、旅客機常連客に対して、安い料金で幅の広い席を提供している。

解法➡ 「大手航空会社は、より広い…を提供している」という意味だから、空欄には array「列、ずらりと並んだもの」が適切である。(A) ally は「同盟国、同盟者」、(B) allay は「(不安・疑い) を鎮める」、(C) alley は「(狭い) 裏通り」という意味である。

覚えてトクする語彙

statistic 名 統計項目 ★★★
statistician 名 統計家 ★★★
statistical 形 統計の ★★★
householder 名 世帯主 ★★★
household goods 名 家庭必需品 ★★★
on the house 熟 店のおごりで ★★★
bring the house down 熟 聴衆の大喝采を博す ★★★
under house arrest 熟 自宅軟禁されて ★★★
housing 名 住宅事情 ★★★
housing complex 名 住宅団地 ★★★

解答・解説　answer and explanation

Answer (A)　　　　　　　　　　　　　　　　　　　**Key Point** 分数

統計によると、現在、独身の労働者はアメリカの全世帯の3分の1を占める。

解法➡ 分数の読み方は、分子には普通の数、分母には序数で読み、分子が2以上の場合には分母に複数のsをつける。

057

Bedding types are ------- request only and rooms with two double beds cannot accommodate a rollaway.

(A) in
(B) by
(C) into
(D) under

《語彙のヒント》

bedding 名 寝具類 ★★★
[bédiŋ]
accommodate 動 …を収容できる ★★★
[əkάmədèit]
rollaway 名 脚輪のついた折りたたみベッド ★★★
[róuləwèi]

058

Mr. Setten has the experience and ------- to handle a multitude of accounting tasks in our department.

(A) versant
(B) versatile
(C) versatility
(D) versification

《語彙のヒント》

handle 動 …を扱う ★★★
[hǽndl]
accounting 名 会計 ★★★
[əkáuntiŋ]

覚えてトクする語彙

bed wetting 名 おねしょ ★★★
bunk bed 名 2段ベッド ★★★
require 動 …を要する ★★★
requirement 名 要求されること ★★★
requisite 名 必要条件 ★★★
accommodation 名 《通常複数形で》宿泊施設 ★★★
accommodating 形 よく世話をする ★★★
accommodator 名 調停者、臨時の家政婦 ★★★
roller coaster 名 ジェットコースター ★★★

解答・解説

Answer (B) **Key Point** 前置詞・熟語

寝具のタイプは依頼によってのみで、ダブルベッド2つの部屋は、折りたたみベッドを収容できません。

解法 by request は「要求、依頼によって」という意味の重要熟語である。at request と言うこともある。

覚えてトクする語彙

account 名 (銀行) 口座、預金 (高) ★★★
accountant 名 会計士 ★★★
account number 名 口座番号 ★★★
account records 名 取引記録 ★★★
accounting department 名 経理部 ★★★
accounting manager 名 経理担当マネージャー ★★★

解答・解説

Answer (C) **Key Point** 単語、品詞

セトン氏には、我々の課で多数の会計の仕事を扱う経験と才能がある。

解法 experience や accounting tasks などの語から、(C) versatility「多才さ」が文脈に当てはまると考えるのが適切である。また、空欄は <experience + and> の後なので、名詞形が来るはず。(A) versant は「山の一斜面」、(B) versatile は (C) versatilility の形容詞形「多芸多才の」、(D) versification は「作詩」という意味である。

059

Detroit, now frequently referred ------- the Motor City, was once known as "Stove Capital of the world."

(A) to
(B) as
(C) as to
(D) to as

《語彙のヒント》

frequently 副 しばしば ★★★
[frí:kwəntli]
stove 名 コンロ ★★★
[stóuv]

060

If you believe you have overpaid your taxes, you have the right to ------- a claim for refund.

(A) fill
(B) file
(C) feel
(D) fillet

《語彙のヒント》

overpay 動 …を余分に払う ★★★
[òuvərpéi]
claim 名 支払い要求、要求 ★★★
[kléim]
refund 名 払い戻し ★★★
[rí:fʌnd]

覚えてトクする語彙

frequency 名 しばしば起こること、周波数 ★★★
frequent 形 たびたび起こる ★★★
frequent flyer 名 (航空会社の) 頻繁利用客 ★★★
worldwide 副 世界で ★★★
for (all) the world 熟 (否定文で) 決して、絶対に ★★★
give the world to do 熟 どんなことがあっても…したい ★★★
on top of the world 熟 とても幸せな、有頂天で ★★★
a world of difference 熟 大きな違い、月とスッポン ★★★
out of this [the] world 熟 とびきりすばらしい ★★★
set the world on fire 熟 世間をあっと言わせる ★★★

解答・解説

Answer (D) **Key Point▶** 前置詞

デトロイトは今ではモーターシティーとよく言われるが、かつては「世界のコンロ都市」として知られていた。

解法▶ 「~と言われている、呼ばれている」は、referred to as ~ である。

覚えてトクする語彙

overhaul 動 …を徹底的に調査する ★★★
override 動 …を却下する ★★★
overthrow 動 …を倒す ★★★
overtake 動 …に追いつく、追いつき追い越す ★★★
feel cheap 熟 決まり悪く思う、まごつく《about》 ★★★
feel ~ in one's bones 熟 …という予感がする ★★★
feel like a million dollars 熟 素敵な気分になる ★★★
feel blue 熟 憂うつである ★★★
feel for ~ 熟 …を手探りで探す ★★★
feel free to do 熟 遠慮なく…する、自由に…する ★★★

解答・解説

Answer (B) **Key Point▶** 単語

もしあなたが税金を払いすぎたと思ったら、あなたには払い戻しの要求を提出する権利がある。

解法▶ 「払い戻しのための支払い要求を申し立てる権利」と解釈すれば、(B) file 「…を提出する」が文脈にぴったりくる。(D) fillet は「(魚・肉の) 骨の無い切り身、ヒレ肉」である。

061

The average German drinks 35% more beer than his Japanese -------.

(A) counter
(B) encounter
(C) counteract
(D) counterpart

《語彙のヒント》

average 形 平均的な ★★★
[ǽvəridʒ]

062

All 97 guest rooms and suites in our hotel are beautifully decorated and offer many in-room -------.

(A) amity
(B) amenities
(C) amnesties
(D) animosity

《語彙のヒント》

suite 名 スイートルーム ★★★
[swíːt]
decorate 動 …を飾る ★★★
[dékərèit]
in-room 形 室内の ★★★
[ínrùːm]

覚えてトクする語彙

on [the, an] average 熟 平均して ★★★
draft beer 名 生ビール ★★★
lager beer 名 ラガービール（加熱殺菌したもの） ★★★
beer belly 名 ビール腹 ★★★
brew 動 ビールなどを醸造する ★★★
brewery 名 （ビールなどの）醸造所 ★★★
brewer 名 ビール醸造人（会社） ★★★
counterfeit 形 本物でない ★★★
countercharge 名 反論 ★★★
countersign 動 （認証のために文書）に連署する ★★★

解答・解説 answer and explanation

Answer (D)　　　　　　　　　　　　　　　　**Key Point**　単語

平均的なドイツ人は、平均的な日本人よりも 35％多くビールを飲む。

解法⇒ counterpart「対をなすものの片方、対応物」は、one に近い代名詞的な働きをし、「よく似た人 [もの]、同等物」の意味を表す。(A) counter は「カウンター、勘定台」、(B) encounter は「（特に偶然の）出会い、遭遇」、(C) counteract は「…に反対に作用する」という意味である。

覚えてトクする語彙

decoration 名 飾りつけ ★★★
decorative 形 装飾の ★★★
decor 名 （部屋・建物の）装飾様式 ★★★
in-house 形 社内の ★★★
in-house training 名 社内教育 ★★★
indoor 形 屋内の ★★★
outdoor 形 屋外の ★★★

解答・解説 answer and explanation

Answer (B)　　　　　　　　　　　　　　　　**Key Point**　単語

当ホテルの 97 の客室とスイートルームは、美しく装飾され、多くの室内備品がそろえてあります。

解法⇒ ホテルの部屋の話という文脈から、(B) amenities「備品、設備」が正解である。(A) amity は「（特に国家間の）友好、親善」、(C) amnesty は「恩赦」、(D) animosity は「悪意、敵意」という意味である。

063

The solid gain in core sales ------- suggest that consumers continue to underpin the economy, despite weaker confidence.

(A) is
(B) are
(C) do
(D) does

《語彙のヒント》

solid 形 堅実な ★★★
[sálid]
underpin 動 …を下から支える ★★★
[ʌ̀ndərpín]
confidence 名 自信、確信、信用、信頼 ★★★
[kánfədəns]

064

Eleven people ------- and 41 displaced after a four-alarm fire engulfed an apartment complex early Monday.

(A) injured
(B) injury
(C) were injured
(D) were injuring

《語彙のヒント》

displace 動 …を移す、退去させる ★★★
[displéis]
four-alarm fire 名 危険度大の火災（alarm の段階が5を最高に、上にいくにつれ、重くなってくる） ★★★
[fɔ́:rəlɑ̀:rm fáiər]
engulf 動 （火・波・戦火などが）…を巻き込む ★★★
[ingʌ́lf]

第1章 ● パート5 短文穴埋め問題

覚えてトクする語彙

solidity 名 堅いこと ★★★
solidify 動 (液体状のもの)を凝固させる ★★★
solidarity 名 団結、結束 ★★★
undercut 動 …よりも安く売る ★★★
understate 動 …を控えめに述べる ★★★
confiding 形 信じやすい ★★★
confident 形 自信のある ★★★
confidential 形 秘密の、(文書が)機密の ★★★
confidentially 副 ないしょで ★★★

解答・解説

Answer (D) **Key Point** 動詞

核となる売り上げの堅実な増加は、自信があまりないにもかかわらず、顧客が弊社の経済を支え続けていることを示している。

解法 問題文には動詞 suggest が存在するので (A) is や (B) are を入れることはできない。また、主語 The solid gain が単数であるので、(C) do も当てはまらない。正解は、動詞を強調する助動詞 (D) does である。

覚えてトクする語彙

displacement 名 移動 ★★★
five-star hotel 名 最高級のホテル (5つ星のホテル) ★★★
encode 動 …を暗号化する ★★★
encumber 動 (動作・活動)を妨げる ★★★
endear 動 …を(〜に)慕わせる《to》 ★★★
endow 動 …に基金を寄付する ★★★
enjoin 動 …に申し付ける ★★★
entrench 動 (考え、慣例)をゆるぎないものにする ★★★
environ 動 …を取り巻く ★★★
envisage 動 …を心に描く ★★★

解答・解説

Answer (C) **Key Point** 受動態

月曜の未明、危険度大の火災があるアパートを巻き込んだ後、11人が負傷し41人が退去させられた。

解法 injure は「…を傷つける」という意味の他動詞である。文脈から「11人の人が負傷を受けた」とわかるので、受動態の形をした (C) を選ぶ。

065

World Trade Organization members ------- over a draft treaty to open markets in agricultural goods.

(A) split
(B) slipped
(C) slopped
(D) slammped

《語彙のヒント》

draft 形 草案の ★★★
[dráft]
treaty 名 条約 ★★★
[tríːti]

066

Mutual fund giant Fidelity Investments' annual profit fell 39 percent for the second year ------- a row.

(A) in
(B) at
(C) off
(D) from

《語彙のヒント》

mutual fund 名 投資信託会社 ★★★
[mjúːtʃuəl fʌ́nd]
fidelity 名 （約束・義務などの）厳守、忠誠 ★★★
[fidélət i]
investment 名 投資 ★★★
[invéstmənt]

覚えてトクする語彙

split *one's* sides 熟 笑いこける ★★★
split the difference 熟 妥協する、残りを平等に分ける ★★★
slip up 熟 間違える ★★★
slip *one's* mind 熟 度忘れする ★★★
slippage 名 滑ること ★★★
slippery 形 よく滑る、つるつるする ★★★
sloppy 形 ぞんざいな、だらしない ★★★
Sloppy Joe 名 丸いパンに味付けした牛ひき肉をはさんだ食べ物 ★★★
drafty 形 隙間風の入る ★★★

解答・解説 answer and explanation

Answer (A) **Key Point** 単語

世界貿易機関のメンバーは、農産物の市場開放条約草案をめぐって、意見が半々に分かれた。

解法 ➡ 「世界貿易機関のメンバーが、草案段階の条約をめぐって…」なのだから、「割れた」という意味の (A) split を選ぶ。この場合の split は過去形であり、原形も split「分裂する、割れる」である。ちなみに、slip は「滑る」、slop は「(液体など)をこぼす」、slam は「(戸・窓を) バタン、ピシャリと閉める」という意味である。

覚えてトクする語彙

mutual 形 相互の ★★★
mutuality 名 相互関係 ★★★
mutually 副 互いに ★★★
fund 名 資金 ★★★
funding 名 (…のための) 財源 ★★★
invest 動 …を投資する ★★★
investor 名 投資家 ★★★
annually 副 毎年 ★★★
annual turnover 名 年間取引高 ★★★

解答・解説 answer and explanation

Answer (A) **Key Point** 前置詞、熟語

巨大投資信託会社のフィデリティー・インベストメンツ社の年間収益は、2年連続して39％落ちた。

解法 ➡ in a row は「連続して」という意味の熟語である。

067

Last summer's drought is being blamed ------- another major agricultural disaster.

 (A) on   (B) for
 (C) of   (D) with

《語彙のヒント》

drought 名 干ばつ ★★★
[dráut]
blame 動 …を（～の）せいにする《on, for》 ★★★
[bléim]
disaster 名 災害 ★★★
[dizǽstər]

068

All of the ------- from the various fund raisers will go toward the Nkoma mission Hospital in Malawi.

 (A) process   (B) proceeds
 (C) progress   (D) processors

《語彙のヒント》

fund raiser 名 資金調達者 ★★★
[fʌ́nd rèizər]
mission 名 （教会などの）社会共済施設、使命 ★★★
[míʃən]

覚えてトクする語彙

droughty 形 乾燥した、日照り続きの ★★★
blameful 形 けしからぬ ★★★
blameless 形 非の打ちどころのない ★★★
majority 名 過半数 ★★★
major in ~ 熟 …を専攻する ★★★
agriculture 名 農業 ★★★
agrichemical 名 農薬（= agricultural chemical） ★★★
disastrous 形 災害を引き起こす ★★★

解答・解説

Answer (B)　　　　　　　　　　　　　　**Key Point** 前置詞、熟語

去年の夏の干ばつが、もう1つの主な農業災害の原因だと言われている。

解法➡ blame A for B、blame B on A で「BをAのせいにする」という熟語である。問題文を能動態にして書き換えると、People [= They] blame last summer's drought for another major agricultural disaster. となる。on を使うと、People [= They] blame another major agricultural disaster on last summer's drought. となり、受動態は Another major agricultural disaster is being blamed on last summer's drought. となる。

覚えてトクする語彙

proceeding 名 進行 ★★★
procedure 名 手順 ★★★
procedural 形 手続き上の ★★★
procession 名 行列 ★★★
progressive 形 進歩的な ★★★
progression 名 前進、連続 ★★★
fund-raising 名 資金集め ★★★
missionary 名 宣教師、使節 ★★★

解答・解説

Answer (B)　　　　　　　　　　　　　　**Key Point** 単語

様々な資金調達者からの全収益は、マラウイ共和国のヌコマ社会共済施設病院に行きます。

解法➡ 「資金調達者からの…」なので、「収益」の意味を持つ proceeds を選ぶ。「収益」という意味のときは、the proceeds と通常複数扱いとなる。ちなみに proceed は、名詞では「収益、結果」、動詞では「前進する《to, into》」という意味である。また、process は名詞で「(製造・加工などの) 過程」、動詞で「…を加工する」、progress は名詞で「進歩、発達」、動詞で「進歩する《in》」、processor は「演算処理装置、言語処理プログラム」という意味である。

069

Our firm ------- in 1948 and has enjoyed a high reputation as importers of sundries of all kinds.

- (A) found
- (B) founded
- (C) establishing
- (D) was established

《語彙のヒント》

firm 名 会社 ★★★
[fə́:rm]
reputation 名 評判、世評 ★★★
[règpjutéiʃən]
sundries 名 雑貨 ★★★
[sʌ́ndriz]

070

NT & T toll-free directory operators ------- nearly half a million calls daily from consumers.

- (A) hand
- (B) handy
- (C) handle
- (D) handily

《語彙のヒント》

toll-free 形 フリーダイヤルの ★★★
[tóulfrí:]
directory 名 住所氏名録 ★★★
[diréktəri]

第1章 ● パート5 短文穴埋め問題

覚えてトクする語彙

establishment 名 設立、体制 ★★★
founder 名 創立者 ★★★
foundation 名 基礎、基盤 ★★★
reputable 形 評判のよい ★★★
sundry 形 いろいろな ★★★
sunbathe 動 日光浴をする ★★★
sunburn 名 日焼け(ひりひりしたり、水ぶくれになったりするほどの) ★★★
suntan 名 日焼け(sunburnとちがって炎症にならないくらいの) ★★★
sunstroke 名 日射病 ★★★

解答・解説

Answer (D) **Key Point** 受動態

弊社は1948年に設立され、あらゆる種類の雑貨の輸入商として、高い評価を得ています。

解法⇒ 主語がOur firm「我が社」なので「設立された」と受動態にしなければならない。

覚えてトクする語彙

toll 名 使用料(税) ★★★
tollbooth 名 (橋・道路の)料金所 ★★★
handout 名 プリント、配布物 ★★★
out of hand 熟 即座に ★★★
(at) first hand 熟 直接に ★★★
on *one's* hands 熟 持て余して ★★★
write a good hand 熟 達筆である ★★★
come in handy 熟 役に立つ ★★★

解答・解説

Answer (C) **Key Point** 単語

NT & T社のフリーダイヤルの番号案内オペレーターは、1日に顧客からの50万近くの通話を処理している。

解法⇒ 主語がNT & T toll-free directory operatorsなので、空欄には動詞が入る。「オペレーターが50万近くの通話を…している」のだから、(A) hand「…を手渡す」より、(C) handle「…を処理する」の方が、文脈にあてはまる。なお、(D) handilyという語はなく、(B) handy「手近にある、手ごろで便利な」は副詞もhandy「手近に」である。

071

Poland's unemployment rate ------- a post-communist high of 18.7 percent last month.

 (A) hit   (B) hits
 (C) was hit   (D) which hit

《語彙のヒント》

post-communist 名 共産主義崩壊以後 ★★★
[pòustkámjunist]

072

We will be unable to make shipment as requested if your L/C does not ------- us by the end of this month.

 (A) get   (B) come
 (C) reach   (D) arrive

《語彙のヒント》

shipment 名 船荷、積み荷、発送 ★★★
[ʃípmənt]
L/C 名 信用状 (= letter of credit) ★★★
[élsí:]

第1章 ● パート5 短文穴埋め問題

覚えてトクする語彙

hit it off 熟 うまくやっていく《with》 ★★★
hit *one's* sore spot 熟 …の痛いところを突く ★★★
hit the books 熟 熱心に勉強する ★★★
hit the ceiling 熟 激怒する ★★★
hit the hay [sack] 熟 寝る ★★★
hit the jackpot 熟 大もうけする、大当たりする ★★★
hit the road 熟 出かける、旅に出る ★★★
hit the spot 熟 もってこいだ、スカッとする ★★★
hit on ~ 熟 …を思いつく ★★★
communism 名 共産主義 ★★★

解答・解説 answer and explanation

Answer (A)　　　　　　　　　　　　　　　　***Key Point*** 動詞

ポーランドの失業率は、先月18.7%という共産主義国崩壊以後の最高となった。

解法▶ 問題文の主語は Poland's unemployment rate「失業率」で、それに対する動詞がないので、空欄には動詞が入る。失業率が最高に達したのだから、能動態があてはまる。また、last month「昨月」とあるので、過去形を選ぶ。

覚えてトクする語彙

make a fast buck 熟 あぶく銭を稼ぐ ★★★
make a killing 熟 大もうけする ★★★
make a name (for *oneself*) 熟 有名になる、名をあげる ★★★
make a toast 熟 乾杯のあいさつをする ★★★
make allowance(s) for ~ 熟 …を考慮に入れる ★★★
make a beeline for ~ 熟 一直線に…へ行く ★★★
make do with ~ 熟 …でなんとかすます ★★★
make no bones about ~ 熟 …をためらわない、…に遠慮しない ★★★
ship 動 …を船に積む、(商品)を出荷する ★★★

解答・解説 answer and explanation

Answer (C)　　　　　　　　　　　　　　　　***Key Point*** 動詞

今月末までに信用状が届かなければ、要請されたように発送することができません。

解法▶「信用状が我々に…ならば」という意味なので、reach「…に届く」が正解である。get を入れると、「信用状が我々を手に入れれば」となり、文脈に合わない。come、arrive は自動詞なので、直後に us という目的語が来ることはない。

073

Overall, a good interviewer is a good listener, is open, and ------- a sense of mutual respect and trust.

(A) built
(B) builds
(C) builder
(D) building

《語彙のヒント》

overall 副 全体的に、総合的に ★★★
[óuvəró:l]
respect 名 尊敬 動 …を尊敬する ★★★
[rispékt]
trust 名 信頼 動 …を信頼する ★★★
[trʌ́st]

074

During the last staff meeting, the following five issues came up -------.

(A) addressed
(B) addressing
(C) to address
(D) to be addressed

《語彙のヒント》

issue 名 問題 動 …を出す、発する ★★★
[íʃu:]
come up 熟 (話題が話に) のぼる ★★★
[kʌ́m ʌp]

第1章 ● パート5 短文穴埋め問題

覚えてトクする語彙

build up ~ 熟 …を強める ★★★
make sense 熟 意味をなす、道理にかなっている ★★★
in a sense 熟 ある意味では ★★★
come to *one's* senses 熟 正気を取り戻す ★★★
respectful 形 尊敬の念に満ちた ★★★
respective 形 それぞれの、各自の ★★★
respectively 副 それぞれ ★★★
with respect to ~ 熟 …に関して ★★★
trustworthy 形 (人・情報などが) 信頼できる ★★★
trustee 名 (会社・学校・協会などの) 役員、評議員 ★★★

解答・解説

Answer (B)　　　　　　　　　　　　　　　　　　**Key Point** 並列

総合して、よい聞き手であり、オープンで、互いに尊敬・信頼を築くことができるのが、良いインタビュアーだ。

解法→ 問題文の主語 a good interviewer に対し、動詞が並列されている (is ~, is ~) ので、空欄には動詞 builds を入れる。動詞が A, B, and C の形で並んでいるわけである。

覚えてトクする語彙

at issue 熟 論点になっている ★★★
come about 熟 起こる ★★★
come over 熟 やって来る ★★★
come by ~ 熟 ひょんなことから…を手に入れる ★★★
come down with ~ 熟 …の病気になる ★★★
come from behind 熟 逆転勝ちする ★★★
come in for ~ 熟 …を受ける ★★★
come into ~ 熟 …を相続する ★★★
come to 熟 意識を回復する ★★★
come across ~ 熟 …に偶然出会う ★★★

解答・解説

Answer (D)　　　　　　　　　　　　　　　　　　**Key Point** 動詞

前回のスタッフミーティングで、次の5つの問題が検討された。

解法→ 前置詞の後に、現在分詞や過去分詞が直接来ることはない。問題文は「検討されるべく、5つの議題が持ち上がった」のであるから、受動態を含んだ to 不定詞である (D) が正解である。ちなみに address は、この文脈では「…を検討する、…に取り組む、…を述べる」という意味である。

Chapter1　81

075

The auto parts maker exposed its nearly 3,000 employees to numerous ------- hazards.

(A) safe (B) safer
(C) safety (D) safely

《語彙のヒント》

expose 動 …を（危険などに）さらす ★★★
[ikspóuz]
numerous 形 非常に多い、おびただしい ★★★
[njú:mərəs]
hazard 名 危険、冒険 ★★★
[hǽzərd]

076

As services to the handicapped have increased, ------- the expectations for improvement.

(A) so (B) have
(C) so have (D) have so

《語彙のヒント》

handicapped 形 障害のある、ハンディのある ★★★
[hǽndikæ̀pt]
expectation 名 期待 ★★★
[èkspektéiʃən]
improvement 名 改善 ★★★
[imprú:vmənt]

第1章 ● パート5 短文穴埋め問題

覚えてトクする語彙

automobile 名 《主にアメリカで》自動車（= auto） ★★★
exposure 名 さらすこと、(フィルムの) ひとこま ★★★
exposition 名 （詳細な）解説 ★★★
expository 形 説明的な ★★★
safety belt 名 安全ベルト ★★★
safe-deposit box 名 （ホテルや銀行の）貸金庫 ★★★
play it safe 熟 安全策を取る ★★★
safe and sound 熟 つつがなく ★★★
hazardous 形 危険な ★★★

解答・解説

Answer (C)　　　　　　　　　　　　　　　　　Key Point. 品詞

その自動車部品メーカーは、3000人近い従業員を安全上おびただしい危険にさらした。

解法 (A) や (B) を選ぶと、「安全な危険」となり意味をなさない。(D) は副詞なので、文法的に空欄にあてはまらない。(C) を選ぶと「安全上の危険」となり、意味が通る。この場合の名詞 safety は、名詞 hazards の前に置かれているため、形容詞の働きをしている。

覚えてトクする語彙

serviceable 形 長持ちする、丈夫な ★★★
handicap 名 ハンディキャップ、不利な条件　動 …を不利な立場に立たせる ★★★
on the increase 熟 増加して ★★★
expect 動 …を期待する ★★★
expectant 形 見込みのある ★★★
expectancy 名 見込み ★★★
life expectancy 名 平均寿命 ★★★
when least expected 熟 思いがけないときに ★★★
improve 動 …を改善する ★★★

解答・解説

Answer (C)　　　　　　　　　　　　　　　　　Key Point. 構文

障害者への奉仕活動が増えるにつれ、改善への期待も高まってきている。

解法 as A, so ...の形で「Aにつれて…、Aと同じような方法で…」の意味を表す。A は節が来る。空欄の後には名詞句が来ているので、<so +助動詞＋主語>の形にしなければならないことがわかる。よって、(C) so have が正解となる。

Chapter1　83

077

The role of the sail has been romanticized throughout history in the ------- of war, trade and even science.

(A) rebels (B) realms
(C) regents (D) reprises

《語彙のヒント》

sail 名 航海、船旅、帆船　★★★
[séil]
romanticize 動 …をロマンチックに描く　★★★
[roumæntəsàiz]

078

------- Japan is mountainous, and only about 20 percent of the land is suitable for agriculture.

(A) Almost (B) Almost of
(C) Most of (D) Most of the

《語彙のヒント》

mountainous 形 山の多い　★★★
[máuntənəs]
land 名 陸、土地　動 上陸する、(飛行機が) 着陸する　★★★
[lænd]

第1章 ● パート5 短文穴埋め問題

覚えてトクする語彙

sailor 名 船員 ★★★
romantic 形 恋愛の、空想的な ★★★
romanticism 名 ロマンチックな性格、理想主義傾向 ★★★
romanticist 名 ロマン主義者、夢を追い求める人 ★★★
rebellion 名 反逆、むほん ★★★
rebellious 形 反抗的な、反体制的な ★★★
revolt 名 反抗、反逆、暴動 ★★★
reprisal 名 報復（行為・攻撃） ★★★

解答・解説

Answer （B）　　　　　　　　　　　　　　　**Key Point** 単語

航海の役割は、歴史を通して、戦争・貿易・科学の分野でさえ、ロマンチックに描かれてきた。

解法▶ 「戦争・貿易・科学の…」なのだから、(B) realms「分野、領域」が意味的にあてはまる。rebel は「反逆者、むほん人」、regent は「（米国・カナダの州立大学・教育機関の）理事、評議員」、reprise は名詞で「《通常複数形で》（土地などの）年間必要経費」、動詞で「…を反復する」という意味である。

覚えてトクする語彙

landing 名 上陸、着陸 ★★★
landowner 名 土地所有者、地主 ★★★
landlord 名 家主 ★★★
landslide 名 地すべり、がけ崩れ ★★★
landfill 名 埋立地 ★★★
landmark 名 画期的な出来事、（航行や旅人にとっての）目じるし ★★★
landmine 名 地雷 ★★★
landscape 名 （陸の）風景 ★★★
land on *one's* feet 熟 見事に切り抜ける ★★★
live on [off] the fat of the land 熟 ぜいたくに暮らす ★★★

解答・解説

Answer （C）　　　　　　　　　　　　　　　**Key Point** 名詞、冠詞

日本は山が多く、たった20％の土地しか農業に適していない。

解法▶ almost は副詞なので、その後に名詞（Japan）は続かない。また、副詞の後に前置詞を持ってきて almost of という言い方はできない。Japan は固有名詞なので、その前に the は不必要である。ここは唯一、Most of Japan ～の形が正しい。

079

A textile plant worker ------- was burned over 90 percent of his body last week died this morning.

 (A) who   (B) which
 (C) whom   (D) where

《語彙のヒント》

textile 名 織物 ★★★
[tékstail]
burn 動 …を燃やす、やけどをさせる ★★★
[bə́ːrn]

080

Legislatures pass many laws that apply only to businesses and individuals, but ------- apply specifically to governments.

 (A) one   (B) another
 (C) some   (D) the other

《語彙のヒント》

legislature 名 議会、立法府 ★★★
[lédʒislèitʃər]
specifically 副 明確に、限定して、特に ★★★
[spisífikəli]

第1章 ● パート5 短文穴埋め問題

覚えてトクする語彙

burner 名 焼却装置 ★★★
burned-out 形 燃え尽きた、(人が) 疲れきった ★★★
burn *one's* fingers 熟 痛い目にあう ★★★
burn the midnight oil 熟 夜遅くまで頑張る ★★★
burn a hole in *one's* pocket 熟 金がすぐに出ていってしまう ★★★
burn up the road 熟 突っ走る ★★★
on the back burner 熟 ほとんど注目されずに ★★★
die hard 熟 (習慣・感情が) なかなかなくならない ★★★
die in the saddle 熟 仕事中に死ぬ ★★★
die [wither] on the vine 熟 実を結ばずに終わる ★★★

解答・解説　answer and explanation

Answer (A)　　　***Key Point*** 関係詞

先週、体全体の90%をやけどした繊維工場の労働者は、今朝亡くなった。

解法⇒ 先行詞が A textile plant worker「繊維工場の労働者」と「人」であり、労働者自身がやけどを負ったのだから、関係代名詞 who を選ぶ。

覚えてトクする語彙

legislate 動 法律を制定する ★★★
legislation 名 立法行為 ★★★
pass out 熟 意識を失う ★★★
pass the buck to ~ 熟 …に責任を転嫁する ★★★
pass away 熟 亡くなる ★★★
pass for ~ 熟 …をして通用する、…で通っている ★★★
pass up ~ 熟 …を見逃す、拒絶する ★★★
specific 形 特定の、一定の ★★★
specify 動 …を明確に述べる ★★★
specification 名 詳細、《複数形で》仕様書 ★★★

解答・解説　answer and explanation

Answer (C)　　　***Key Point*** 代名詞

議会は会社や個人に適応する多くの法律を可決するが、政府に限定して適応する法律もいくつかある。

解法⇒ 空欄には、その後の動詞 apply に対する主語が入る。(C) some 以外の選択肢は、すべて単数形なのであてはまらない。some は many laws に対して用いられており、some laws のことを意味していることがわからなければならない。

081

The nation's largest radio station operator has posted a fourth-quarter profit in contrast ------- a loss a year ago.

(A) of
(B) to
(C) for
(D) from

《語彙のヒント》

operator 名 経営者、(機械などの) 操作者 ★★★
[ápərèitər]
post 動 …を公表する、(掲示) をはる ★★★
[póust]
contrast 名 対照、対比 ★★★
[kántræst]

082

At least one in ten voters nationwide cast ballots in the last ------- election on electronic voting machines.

(A) preside
(B) president
(C) presidency
(D) presidential

《語彙のヒント》

cast 動 …を投げる ★★★
[kæst]
ballot 名 投票 ★★★
[bælət]
electronic 形 電子の ★★★
[ilektránik]

覚えてトクする語彙

operate [動] …を操作する、経営する ★★★
operation [名] 手術、事業、作用 ★★★
operational [形] 使用できる、操作上の ★★★
poster [名] ポスター ★★★
contrary [形] 正反対の、相容れない ★★★
contrastive [形] 対照的な ★★★
on the contrary [熟] それどころか ★★★
lose [動] …を失う ★★★
loser [名] 敗者 ★★★

解答・解説 answer and explanation

Answer (B) **Key Point** 熟語

その国で一番大きいラジオ局の経営者は、前年の損益とは対照的に、25％の利益増を公表した。

解法➡ in [by] contrast to ～は「…とは対照的に」という重要熟語である。TOEICによく出る熟語なので前置詞に注意して、しっかり覚えておこう。

覚えてトクする語彙

vote [動] 投票をする ★★★
elect [動] …を選挙する ★★★
elective [形] 選挙の、(大学で) 選択の ★★★
electronic mail [名] 電子メール (= email) ★★★
electronics [名] (単数扱いで) 電子工学 ★★★
electron [名] 電子 ★★★
electricity [名] 電気 ★★★
electric [形] 電気の ★★★
electrocardiogram [名] 心電図 ★★★

解答・解説 answer and explanation

Answer (D) **Key Point** 品詞

少なくとも国中の選挙民10人に1人が、前回の大統領選で、電子投票機により投票した。

解法➡ 「大統領選」は、presidential election という。preside は「司会をする」、presidency は「大統領の地位、職務」という意味である。

083

Friendly Corp. is still ------- how many jobs will be cut at its corporate headquarters.

(A) determine
(B) determined
(C) determining
(D) determination

《語彙のヒント》

determine 動 …を決定する ★★★
[ditə́ːrmin]

headquarters 名 本社、本部 ★★★
[hédkwɔ̀ːrtərz]

084

This is perhaps one of ------- interesting, exciting and profitable businesses you will ever see.

(A) more
(B) most
(C) a most
(D) the most

《語彙のヒント》

profitable 形 利益になる ★★★
[práfitəbl]

第1章 ● パート5 短文穴埋め問題

覚えてトクする語彙

determined [形] （性格・表情などが）決然とした、断固とした ★★★
determination [名] 決定、決心 ★★★
cut down on ~ [熟] …を減らす ★★★
cut no ice [熟] 効果がない ★★★
cut a figure [熟] 注意を引く ★★★
cut corners [熟] 手を抜く、近道する ★★★
cut loose [熟] 息抜きをする《from》 ★★★
be cut out for ~ [熟] …に適している ★★★
a cut above ~ [熟] …より一段優れて ★★★
be cut up [熟] 悲しむ、傷つく ★★★

解答・解説

Answer （C） **Key Point**, 品詞

フレンドリー社は、本社でいくつの仕事がカットされるか、まだ取り決めている最中だ。

解法→ 空欄の前に is があるので、（A） determine はあてはまらない。空欄の後は how many ～なので、（D） determination だと、つながらない。意味的に「フレンドリー社は決定している」が適当であろうから、進行形の（C） determining が正解である。

覚えてトクする語彙

foremost [形] 先頭の、真っ先の、最も重要な ★★★
first and foremost [熟] 真っ先に、いの一番に ★★★
wrong end foremost [熟] 前後を逆に、あべこべに ★★★
no more than [熟] わずか ★★★
not more than [熟] せいぜい、多くて ★★★
more often than not [熟] しばしば ★★★
excitement [名] 興奮 ★★★
excite [動] …を刺激する ★★★
profit [名] 利益 ★★★
profitless [形] 利益のない ★★★

解答・解説

Answer （D） **Key Point**, 比較

これはおそらく、あなたの知る限りもっとも興味深く刺激的で利益のあるビジネスになるだろう。

解法→ one of ------ とあるので、最上級を選ぶ。最上級には、the が必要である。

085

Michael Morgan will retire as chairman and director in May and will ------- by CEO John Moore.

(A) replace
(B) replacing
(C) be replaced
(D) be replacing

《語彙のヒント》

chairman 名 会長、議長、司会者 ★★★
[tʃɛ́ərmən]
director 名 取締役、指導者、(会社の) 重役 ★★★
[diréktər]
CEO 名 最高経営責任者 (= chief executive officer) ★★★
[síːóu]

086

Unions tend to negotiate wage levels that are higher than those ------- to nonunion workers in similar circumstances.

(A) pay
(B) paid
(C) paying
(D) to pay

《語彙のヒント》

union 名 組合、結合 ★★★
[júːnjən]
negotiate 動 …を交渉する ★★★
[nigóuʃièit]
wage 名 賃金 ★★★
[wéidʒ]

第1章 ● パート5 短文穴埋め問題

覚えてトクする語彙

direct 動 …を導く ★★★
chief 形 最高位の、長 ★★★
executive 名 経営幹部、重役 ★★★
officer 名 役人、(団体・企業の) 役員、警官 ★★★
official 名 (政府の) 役人、公務員、官僚 ★★★
officially 副 職務上、公式に ★★★

解答・解説

Answer (C)　　　　　　　　　　　　　　**Key Point,** 受動態

マイケル・モーガンは、5月に会長・取締役を退職し、最高経営責任者のジョン・ムーアが後を引き継ぐ。

解法→ 空欄の後に by があるので、受動態である可能性が高い。意味をとってみると、「マイケル・モーガンがジョン・ムーアによって…」なのだから、「置き換えられる」という意味の (C) be replaced が適切である。

覚えてトクする語彙

tendency 名 傾向 ★★★
negotiation 名 交渉 ★★★
negotiator 名 交渉者 ★★★
negotiable 形 交渉の余地がある ★★★
minimum wage 名 最低賃金 ★★★
circumscribe 動 …を制限する ★★★
circumference 名 円周 ★★★
circumvent 動 (問題・失敗) を逃れる ★★★
circumspect 形 慎重な ★★★
circumlocution 名 まわりくどい表現 ★★★

解答・解説

Answer (B)　　　　　　　　　　　　　　**Key Point,** 分詞

組合は、似た状況で組合に加入していない労働者に払われているより高い賃金レベルを得ようと交渉する傾向にある。

解法→ 空欄直前の those は wage levels のことであり、wage levels は「払っている」のではなく「払われる」のだから、paid と受動態の意味を表す過去分詞にする。

087

It appears that non-profit organizations principally have a common objective to aid people who are in -------.

　　(A) need　　　　　　(B) needy
　　(C) needed　　　　　(D) needing

《語彙のヒント》

principally 副 主に ★★★
[prínsəpəli]
objective 名 目的　形 客観的な ★★★
[əbdʒéktiv]
aid 動 …を援助する　名 援助 ★★★
[éid]

088

US Airways will begin a daily nonstop flight between Charlotte ------- Mexico City this fall.

　　(A) or　　　　　　(B) and
　　(C) but　　　　　(D) nor

《語彙のヒント》

daily 形 毎日の ★★★
[déili]
flight 名 定期航空便 ★★★
[fláit]

第1章 ● パート5 短文穴埋め問題

覚えてトクする語彙

appearance 名 出現、外観、容姿 ★★★
in appearance 熟 見かけは ★★★
principal 形 主な、主要な 名 (団体の) 長、校長 ★★★
principle 名 原理、原則 ★★★
in principle 熟 原則的に ★★★
object 名 物、物体 ★★★
objection 名 異議、反対 ★★★
aide 名 助手、(大統領の) 補佐官 ★★★
be in need of ~ 熟 …を必要としている ★★★
if need be 熟 必要とあらば ★★★

解答・解説 answer and explanation

Answer (A) ***Key Point*** 品詞
非営利団体は主として、困難な状況にある人を援助することを共通の目的としているようだ。
解法 needy は「ひどく貧乏な」の意味を表す形容詞なので、needy を使うなら、直前の in は要らない。前置詞 in の後なので、名詞の need にする。in need は「困窮している、困っている」の意味の熟語として覚えておくとよい。

覚えてトクする語彙

weekly 形 毎週の ★★★
monthly 形 毎月の ★★★
yearly 形 毎年の ★★★
flight number 名 (航空便の) 便名 ★★★
flight recorder 名 飛行記録装置 (= black box) ★★★
flight path 名 飛行経路 ★★★
fright 名 恐怖 ★★★
between ourselves 熟 ここだけの話だが ★★★
read between the lines 熟 言外の意味を読み取る ★★★
between *one's* teeth 熟 小声で ★★★

解答・解説 answer and explanation

Answer (B) ***Key Point*** 熟語
US 航空会社は、この秋、シャーロットとメキシコシティー間の直行便を毎日運航します。
解法 between A and B で「A と B の間で」という決まった言い方である。

089

The zoo exhibits have been designed to ------- simulate life in the wild that provides a stimulating environment for the animals.

(A) close
(B) closed
(C) closing
(D) closely

《語彙のヒント》

exhibit 名 展示、提示 動 …を展示する ★★★
[igzíbit]
simulate 動 …をまねる ★★★
[símjulèit]
stimulating 形 刺激的な ★★★
[stímjulèitiŋ]

090

The airline faces almost imminent liquidation if it is not permitted ------- the pension plan for its 6,000 pilots.

(A) terminate
(B) terminated
(C) terminating
(D) to terminate

《語彙のヒント》

imminent 形 (悪いことが) 今にも起ころうとしてる、切迫した ★★★
[ímənənt]
liquidation 名 (会社などの) 破産、解散 ★★★
[lìkwidéiʃən]
pension 名 年金、恩給 ★★★
[pénʃən]

第1章 ● パート5 短文穴埋め問題

覚えてトクする語彙

exhibition 名 展覧会、展示会 ★★★
exhibitor 名 (展覧会などの) 参加者 ★★★
exhibitive 形 展示の ★★★
simulation 名 シミュレーション、ふりをすること ★★★
simulated 形 模擬の ★★★
provision 名 供給、用意 ★★★
provided 接 (…という) 条件で、もし…ならば (= providing) ★★★
stimulate 動 …を刺激する ★★★
stimulation 名 刺激 ★★★
stimulus 名 励み、刺激物 ★★★

解答・解説 answer and explanation

Answer (D)　　　　　　　　　　　　　　　　　　　　　　　**Key Point.** 品詞

その動物園は、動物に刺激ある環境を与える野生の生活によく似せた造りになっている。

解法▶ designed to の to は不定詞なので、simulate は動詞である。空欄部分は動詞 simulate にかかっていくので、副詞形 closely にしなくてはいけない。

覚えてトクする語彙

imminence 名 差し迫った状況 ★★★
liquidate 動 (会社が) 破産する、(倒産会社が) 負債を清算する ★★★
liquidator 名 清算人 ★★★
liquid 形 流動性の、(資産・証券などが) 現金化しやすい ★★★
liquidity 名 換金性 ★★★
permission 名 許可 ★★★
termination 名 終了、終結 ★★★
terminator 名 終結させる人 ★★★
terminal 形 (病気が) 末期的な、絶望的な ★★★
pensioner 名 年金受給者 ★★★

解答・解説 answer and explanation

Answer (D)　　　　　　　　　　　　　　　　　　　　　**Key Point.** 不定詞

その航空会社は、もし操縦士6000人の年金計画打ち切りの許可が出なければ、破産に追い込まれるという緊迫した状況に直面している。

解法▶ 「(人に) …することを許す」は <permit + 目的語 + to *do*> であり、問題文では受動態の文中で用いられているので、permitted の後は不定詞の to terminate とすべきである。ちなみに terminate は「…を終わらせる」という意味である。

091

We strive to support each individual with the training and opportunities essential to progressive career -------.

(A) grow
(B) grown
(C) growth
(D) growing

《語彙のヒント》

strive 動 努力する、懸命に試みる ★★★
[stráiv]
opportunity 名 好機、機会 ★★★
[ὰpərtjú:nəti]
progressive 形 進歩的な、進歩する、向上する ★★★
[prəgrésiv]

092

Researchers are offering a computerized screening tool to high schools in hopes of ------- teenagers suffering from depression.

(A) identify
(B) identity
(C) identifying
(D) identification

《語彙のヒント》

computerized 形 コンピュータ化された ★★★
[kəmpjú:təràizd]
screening 名 ふるい分け ★★★
[skrí:niŋ]
depression 名 うつ病、憂うつ、不景気 ★★★
[dipréʃən]

第1章 ● パート5 短文穴埋め問題

覚えてトクする語彙

individuality 名 個性 ★★★
individualism 名 個人主義 ★★★
individualist 名 個人主義者 ★★★
individualize 動 …の個性を際立たせる ★★★
opportune 形 適切な、好都合の ★★★
opportunism 名 便宜主義、日和見主義 ★★★
opportunistic 形 便宜主義的な、日和見主義的な ★★★
progression 名 前進、発達 ★★★
progress 動 進行する、前進する ★★★
progress report 名 (仕事の) 進行報告書 ★★★

解答・解説

Answer (C) **Key Point** 品詞

我々は、進歩するキャリアアップに欠かせないトレーニングと機会を提供し、各個人をサポートする努力をしている。

解法→ to progressive career 〜の to は前置詞で、これは前置詞句であるので、空欄には名詞 growth を入れる。career growth で「キャリアアップ」くらいの意味である。

覚えてトクする語彙

computerize 動 …をコンピュータ化する ★★★
screen 動 …をふるいにかける、選別する ★★★
tool box 名 道具箱 ★★★
tool kit 名 工具セット ★★★
identification card 名 身分証明書 (= ID card) ★★★
identical 形 同一の、まったく一致した ★★★
suffering 名 苦しみ、苦痛 ★★★
depress 動 …を憂うつにさせる ★★★
depressing 形 憂うつな、気のめいるような ★★★
depressed 形 元気のない ★★★

解答・解説

Answer (C) **Key Point** 動名詞

研究者は、うつ病にかかっているティーンエイジャーの識別を目的に、高校にコンピュータ化されたスクリーニングツールを提供している。

解法→ 空欄は前置詞 of のすぐ後なので、(C) identifying と動名詞にする。(B) identity「同一性」と (D) identification「識別」も名詞だが、意味上不適切である。

093

Hokkaido is Japan's northernmost island, ------- heavy snowfall is prevalent and winter is the longest season of the year.

(A) that
(B) which
(C) whose
(D) where

《語彙のヒント》

northernmost 形 最北の ★★★
[nɔ́ːrðərnmòust]
snowfall 名 降雪（量） ★★★
[snóufɔ̀ːl]
prevalent 形 広く行き渡った、流行した ★★★
[prévələnt]

094

Some jobs such as accountant, cashier and bank teller, provide more opportunity for embezzlement than other jobs where the employee has ------- contact with money.

(A) lot
(B) few
(C) little
(D) many

《語彙のヒント》

cashier 名 レジ係、現金出納係 ★★★
[kæʃíər]
bank teller 名 銀行の現金出納係 ★★★
[bǽŋk télər]
embezzlement 名 着服、横領、使い込み ★★★
[imbézlmənt]

第1章 ● パート5 短文穴埋め問題

覚えてトクする語彙

northern 形 北の ★★★
northern hemisphere 名 北半球 ★★★
northbound 形 北行きの、北へ向かう ★★★
southernmost 形 最南（端）の ★★★
snowbound 形 雪にとじこめられた ★★★
snowball 動 雪だるま式に増える ★★★
snowman 名 雪だるま ★★★
snowstorm 名 吹雪 ★★★
prevail 動 広く一般に存在する、普及している ★★★
prevailing 形 （意見などが）行き渡った、支配的な ★★★

解答・解説　answer and explanation

Answer （D）　　　　　　　　　　　　　　**Key Point** 関係副詞

北海道は、日本の最北の島で、大雪が広く降り、1年で冬が一番長い。

解法➡ コンマ以下は、and in Hokkaido heavy snowfall is prevalent and winter is the longest season of the year と書き直すことができる。よって、関係副詞 where が適切である。which だと、in Hokkaido の in が入らないので誤りとなる。

覚えてトクする語彙

cash 名 現金　動 （小切手や為替など）を現金に換える ★★★
cash in on ～ 熟 …を利用する、つけ込む ★★★
bank book 名 銀行通帳 ★★★
bank note 名 銀行券、紙幣 ★★★
bank account 名 銀行預金残高 ★★★
bank statement 名 （銀行から顧客に送られてくる）口座収支報告書 ★★★
embezzle 動 （…から）横領する《from》 ★★★
few and far between 熟 ごく少ない ★★★
quite a few 熟 相当たくさんの ★★★

解答・解説　answer and explanation

Answer （C）　　　　　　　　　　　　　　**Key Point** 名詞、形容詞

会計士・レジ係、銀行の出納係などの仕事は、従業員がお金を扱うことがほとんどないほかの仕事より、着服する機会が多く存在する。

解法➡ contact「接触」は不可算名詞なので、little「ほとんどない」を用いる。few と many は可算名詞に用いる。lot の場合は、a lot of か lots of とすべきである。

Chapter1 ■■■ 101

095

Global Corp. posted a ------- four-percent increase in profit for the fourth quarter, boosted by increased earnings from its credit card division.

(A) modest
(B) modesty
(C) modestly
(D) moderately

《語彙のヒント》

global 形 全世界の、地球上の、全体的な ★★★
[glóubəl]
boost 動 …を引き上げる、押し上げる ★★★
[búːst]
earnings 名 利益、収入 ★★★
[ə́ːrniŋz]

096

The company has achieved profitable growth averaging 25 percent each year and a ------- market share in Western Canada.

(A) commando
(B) commandeer
(C) commanding
(D) commandment

《語彙のヒント》

average 動 …を平均する ★★★
[ǽvəridʒ]
market share 名 (ある製品の) 市場占有率 ★★★
[máːrkit ʃέər]

覚えてトクする語彙

global warming 名 地球温暖化 ★★★
globalism 名 世界化 ★★★
globalize 動 …を世界化する、国際化する ★★★
globe 名 地球 ★★★
booster 名 援助者、後援者 ★★★
earning 名 働いて収入を得ること ★★★
earn 動 (金)を稼ぐ、もうける ★★★
earner 名 稼ぎ手 ★★★
earned income 名 勤労所得 ★★★

解答・解説 answer and explanation

Answer (A)　　　　　　　　　　　　　　　**Key Point** 品詞

グローバル・コーポレーションは、クレジットカード部門からの収益増加により利益が上がった第4四半期の収益を、控えめに4%の増加と公表した。

解法▶ 空欄には、four-percent increase「4%の増加」という名詞句にかかっていく形容詞 modest が適切。modesty は名詞で「控えめ、謙虚」という意味であり、副詞 moderately は「適度に」という意味である。

覚えてトクする語彙

yearly 形 1年の 副 年1度 ★★★
year-end 形 年末の ★★★
marketing 名 マーケティング ★★★
marketable 形 市場向きの、よく売れる ★★★
market-driven 形 市場(需要)先導の ★★★
market price 名 市場価格、相場 ★★★
market research [survey] 名 市場調査 ★★★
market value 名 市場価値 ★★★

解答・解説 answer and explanation

Answer (C)　　　　　　　　　　　　　　　**Key Point** 品詞、単語

その会社は、毎年平均25%の収益増加と西カナダでの圧倒的な市場占有率を成し遂げてきた。

解法▶ 空欄の前には冠詞 a が、後には名詞 market share があるので、ここは形容詞 commanding「圧倒的な、優勢な」が適切である。その他の選択肢の意味は、(A) commando「特殊部隊」、(B) commandeer「…を奪い取る」、(C) commandment「戒め」である。

097

China Airways Co. expects its net loss this fiscal year to reach 35 billion yuan, ------- twice earlier forecasts, due to industry competition.

(A) near
(B) nearby
(C) nearly
(D) nearness

《語彙のヒント》

net 形 正味の ★★★
[nét]
fiscal year 名 会計年度 ★★★
[fískəl jíər]
forecast 名 予測、予測、予報　動 …を（特に知識に基づいて）予想する、予測する ★★★
[fɔ́:rkæst]

098

Micron Technology Inc., the world's second ------- computer memory chip maker, is laying off 10 percent of its worldwide labor force of over 18,000.

(A) large
(B) larger
(C) largest
(D) as large as

《語彙のヒント》

chip 名 半導体素子、集積回路（= integrated circuit） ★★★
[tʃíp]
lay off ～ 熟 …を一時解雇する ★★★
[léi ɔ́:f]

第1章 ● パート5 短文穴埋め問題

覚えてトクする語彙

billionaire 名 億万長者 ★★★
weather forecast 名 天気予報 ★★★
foresee 動 …を予知する、見越す ★★★
foreseeable 形 予測可能な ★★★

解答・解説

Answer (C)　　　　　　　　　　　　　　　　　***Key Point*** 品詞

中華航空会社は業界内競争のせいで、本会計年度の損失が以前提出された予測のほぼ2倍の350億元に達するであろうと予想している。

解法→ 文意から「ほぼ2倍」という意味なので、「ほぼ、およそ」という意味の副詞形 nearly にする。

覚えてトクする語彙

memorial 形 記念の、追悼の ★★★
memorable 形 記憶すべき、重要な ★★★
memorize 動 …を記憶する、暗記する ★★★
memorization 名 暗記 ★★★
memoir 名 回顧録、回想録 ★★★
memorabilia 名 記憶に値する事柄、品物 ★★★
tip 名 チップ、心づけ ★★★
lay [stop] over 熟 途中下車する ★★★
lay down the law 熟 厳しく正す ★★★
lay the groundwork for 〜 熟 …の根回しをする ★★★

解答・解説

Answer (C)　　　　　　　　　　　　　　　　　***Key Point*** 最上級

マイクロン・テクノロジー社は、世界で2番目に大きいコンピュータ記憶集積回路のメーカーで、世界中にいる1万8000人以上の労働者の10%を一時解雇している。

解法→「世界で2番目に大きい」のだから、large を最上級の largest にする。

099

Weak financial markets are unlikely to impede the U.S. ------- recovery, given signs of strength in the household and banking sectors.

(A) economy
(B) economic
(C) economics
(D) economical

《語彙のヒント》

impede 動 …を遅らせる、妨げる ★★★
[impíːd]
household 形 家庭用の、家族の ★★★
[háushòuld]
sector 名 (産業などの) 活動部門 ★★★
[séktər]

100

Synthetic fabrics which are manufactured or artificial materials are the most ------- used in the clothing industry today.

(A) wide
(B) widen
(C) widest
(D) widely

《語彙のヒント》

synthetic fabric 名 合成繊維 ★★★
[sinθétik fǽbrik]
manufacture 動 …を製造する ★★★
[mæ̀njufǽktʃər]
artificial 形 人工の ★★★
[àːrtəfíʃəl]

覚えてトクする語彙

unlike 形 似ていない、違った ★★★
unlikelihood 名 ありそうもないこと ★★★
impediment 名 妨害、障害 ★★★
recover 動 …を取り戻す、回復する ★★★
householder 名 世帯主、家屋所有者 ★★★
housemaker 名 主婦 (= homemaker) ★★★
housekeeper 名 家政婦、家事をする人 ★★★
housekeeping 名 家計の切り盛り ★★★
housework 名 家事 ★★★

解答・解説

Answer (B) **Key Point** 形容詞、単語

家庭・金融部門に強さが見えてきたことを考えると、金融市場の弱さが合衆国の経済の回復を妨げるとは考えられない。

解法 それぞれの選択肢の意味を確認しておこう。(A) economy は「経済、景気」、(B) economic は「経済の」、(C) economics は「経済学」、(D) economical は「経済的な、節約の」の意味である。空欄の後の recovery「回復」を正しく修飾できるのは、形容詞の economical である。

覚えてトクする語彙

synthetic detergent 名 合成洗剤 ★★★
synthetic rubber 名 合成ゴム ★★★
synthesize 動 …を総合する、合成する ★★★
synthesis 名 総合、統合 ★★★
synthesizer 名 総合する人、シンセサイザー ★★★
fabric conditioner 名 柔軟仕上げ剤 ★★★
manufacturer 名 製造者、メーカー ★★★
artificial intelligence 名 人工知能 (= AI) ★★★
artificial respiration 名 人工呼吸 ★★★
artificiality 名 人為、不自然さ ★★★

解答・解説

Answer (D) **Key Point** 品詞

加工されたり人工的な材料を使った合成繊維は、服飾産業で今日もっとも幅広く使われている。

解法 空欄は直後の過去分詞 used にかかっていくので、widely と副詞形にする必要がある。

101

Gov. Clark's plan to shift state employees' payday to save money in this fiscal year got a cold ------- from Republican lawmakers.

(A) receive
(B) received
(C) receiving
(D) reception

《語彙のヒント》

shift 動 …を移動する、変える ★★★
[ʃíft]
Republican 名 《アメリカの》共和党党員・支持者 ★★★
[ripʌ́blikən]
lawmaker 名 立法者、議員 ★★★
[lɔ́ːmèikər]

102

Our record as oil finders and emphasis on -------, low cost operations create the foundation for excellent growth in shareholder value.

(A) efficiency
(B) efficiencies
(C) efficient
(D) efficiently

《語彙のヒント》

emphasis 名 強調、力説、重要視 ★★★
[émfəsis]
shareholder 名 株主（= stockholder） ★★★
[ʃέərhòuldər]

第1章 ● パート5 短文穴埋め問題

覚えてトクする語彙

Govt. 名 政府（= government） ★★★
shiftwork 名 交替勤務 ★★★
night shift 名 夜勤 ★★★
shift stick 名 ギアレバー ★★★
shifty 形 策に富んだ、ごまかしの多い ★★★
Republican Party 名 《アメリカの》共和党 ★★★
Democratic Party 名 《アメリカの》民主党 ★★★
lawmaking 形 立法の ★★★
law-abiding 形 法律を遵守する ★★★
lawbreaking 形 法律違反の ★★★

解答・解説

Answer (D) **Key Point** 品詞

本会計年度の金を節約するため州労働者の給料日を変更するというクラーク州知事の計画は、共和党議員たちから冷たい目を向けられた。

解法 → 動詞 got の後には目的語となるべき名詞が必要なので、空欄には名詞形 reception が正しい。a cold reception で「冷遇」の意味である。

覚えてトクする語彙

emphasize 動 …を強調する、力説する、重要視する ★★★
emphatic 形 強調された、強い調子の ★★★
valuable 形 価値のある、評価できる ★★★
valueless 形 無価値な、つまらない ★★★
valuate 動 …を評価する、査定する ★★★
valuation 名 （物の金銭的）評価、査定 ★★★
valuator 名 評価者、価格査定官 ★★★
value-added 名 付加価値 ★★★
value pricing 名 お得値段設定 ★★★

解答・解説

Answer (C) **Key Point** 品詞

我々の石油発見者としての経歴と、能率的な低コスト作業の強調は、株主の評価を高く伸ばすための基盤を作り出している。

解法 → emphasis on の後には名詞句がくるべきであり、efficient, low cost operations が適切な形である。形容詞 efficient「能率的な、有能な」と形容詞 low の間のコンマは and の働きをしている。

Chapter1 ■■■ 109

103

A San Diego-area auto body repair company has reached an overtime pay ------- with the Department of Labor.

(A) settle (B) settled
(C) settling (D) settlement

《語彙のヒント》

repair 名 修理 動 …を修理する ★★★
[ripéər]
overtime 名 超過時間、超過勤務時間 ★★★
[óuvərtàim]

104

Snider Inc. has signed a letter of ------- with FAO Inc. to operate toy shops in most of the 245 stores in its department store division.

(A) intent (B) intensity
(C) intention (D) intending

《語彙のヒント》

sign 動 …に署名する、…とサインして契約する ★★★
[sáin]

第1章 ● パート5 短文穴埋め問題

覚えてトクする語彙

repairman 名 (自動車の) 修理工、修繕屋 ★★★
overhead 名 一般経費 ★★★
overrun 名 在庫品 ★★★
overdose 名 (薬の) 飲みすぎ ★★★
overissue 名 (株券・債権などの) 過剰発行 ★★★
overproduction 名 過剰生産 ★★★
overweight 名 超過重量、太りすぎ ★★★
overuse 名 酷使、乱用 ★★★
oversight 名 見過ごし、不注意 ★★★
overview 名 概観、総覧 ★★★

解答・解説

Answer (D) **Key Point** 品詞

サンディエゴ地域の自動車車体修理会社は、労働省と超過勤務手当ての合意に至った。

解法 an overtime pay ~ は、動詞 has reached の目的語にあたるので、空欄には動詞 settle「…を確定する、決める」の名詞形である settlement を入れる。

覚えてトクする語彙

signature 名 署名 ★★★
autograph 名 有名人のサイン ★★★
signatory 形 署名した ★★★
signal 名 信号、合図 ★★★
letterhead 名 レターヘッド (便せん上部に印刷した個人・会社などの住所名前など) ★★★
letter of credit 名 信用状 (= L.C., L/C) ★★★
letter opener 名 開封用ペーパーナイフ ★★★
intentionally 副 意図して、故意に ★★★

解答・解説

Answer (A) **Key Point** 単語

スナイダー社は、デパート部門245店のほとんどの玩具店舗を経営するため、FAO社との意向書にサインした。

解法 文脈から、ここは「意向書」を意味する目的語がくると判断し、a letter of intent とする。(B) intensity「強度、激しさ」と (C) intention「意図、決意」の意味も確認しておこう。

105

H & R Block Inc. reported record earnings and revenues for its third quarter, thanks largely ------- a strong performance in its mortgage business.

(A) in
(B) of
(C) to
(D) for

《語彙のヒント》

revenue 名 収益、売り上げ、(国の) 歳入 ★★★
[révənjùː]
performance 名 運用業績、パフォーマンス、履行 ★★★
[pərfɔ́ːrməns]

106

Sunrise Corp. said Thursday its profit more than ------- in the fourth quarter despite a slight decline in sales.

(A) triple
(B) tripled
(C) triplet
(D) triplex

《語彙のヒント》

profit 名 収益、利益 ★★★
[práfit]
quarter 名 四半期、4分の1 ★★★
[kwɔ́ːrtər]

第1章 ● パート5 短文穴埋め問題

覚えてトクする語彙

annual revenue 名 年間売上高、年商 ★★★
domestic revenue 名 国内売上 ★★★
international revenue 名 海外売上（= overseas revenue）★★★
operating revenue 名 営業収益 ★★★
revenue growth 名 増収、売上増 ★★★
revenue stamp 名 収入印紙 ★★★
perform 動 （任務など）を成し遂げる、履行する ★★★
performance test 名 性能テスト ★★★
performance appraisal 名 勤務評定 ★★★
performance-related pay 名 能力給 ★★★

解答・解説　answer and explanation

Answer （C）　　　***Key Point***　熟語

Ｈ＆Ｒブロック社は、おもに住宅金融業の効果的な運用業績のおかげで、第３四半期の記録的売り上げ増収を発表した。

解法➡ 熟語 thanks to ～「…のおかげで」の thanks と to の間に副詞の largely が挿入されている。

覚えてトクする語彙

twins 名 双子 ★★★
quadruplets 名 四つ子（= quads）★★★
quintuplets 名 五つ子（= quints）★★★
triangle 名 三角形 ★★★
tricycle 名 三輪車（= trike）★★★
trillion 名 １兆 ★★★
trimester 名 （３学期制の）１学期 ★★★
trio 名 ３つ組、３人組 ★★★

解答・解説　answer and explanation

Answer （B）　　　***Key Point***　動詞

サンライズ社は、売上がわずかに落ちたにもかかわらず、第４四半期の収益が３倍以上になったと、木曜日に報告した。

解法➡ said Thursday の後には that 節がくるはずであるが、問題文には its profit に対する動詞がない。空欄の直前の more than は、この場合、動詞を修飾する副詞なので、「…より以上に」の意味を持つ。よって、空欄には tripled（動詞「３倍になる」の過去形）を入れるとよい。(C) triplet は「三つ子」、(D) triplex は「３階建てのアパート、３部」の意味である。

107

Mr. Kaylor was ------- in designing, creating and implementing the market strategies for our overseas sales department.

(A) instrument
(B) instrumental
(C) instrumentalist
(D) instrumentation

《語彙のヒント》

implement 動 …を実行する、実施する ★★★
[ímpləmənt]
strategy 名 戦略 ★★★
[strǽtədʒi]

108

To make your speech more -------, visual aids should be relevant to your topic and your communicative purpose.

(A) effect
(B) effected
(C) effective
(D) effectively

《語彙のヒント》

visual aids 名 視覚教材、視覚資料 ★★★
[víʒuəl éidz]
relevant 形 関係のある、適切な ★★★
[réləvənt]
purpose 名 目的、用途 ★★★
[pə́ːrpəs]

第1章 ● パート5 短文穴埋め問題

覚えてトクする語彙

designer 名 設計者、デザイナー ★★★
designer label 名 デザイナー・ブランド ★★★
designed 形 故意の、計画的な ★★★
designing 形 ずるい、先見の明のある ★★★
creative 形 創造力のある ★★★
creativity 名 創造性、独創性 ★★★
creation 名 創造、創作 ★★★
implementation 名 実行、実施 ★★★
strategic 形 戦略的な ★★★
strategist 名 策略家 ★★★

解答・解説

Answer (B) 　　　　　　　　　　　　　　　　　　**Key Point** 品詞

ケーラー氏は、我々の海外販売部で、販売戦略の設計・製作・実行に役に立った。

解法▶ (A) instrument は「道具」という可算名詞で冠詞 an が必要であるし、第一、ケーラー氏が道具では意味的におかしい。ここは形容詞の (B) instrumental 「役に立つ」を用いるのが正しい。(C) instrumentalist は「楽器演奏者」、(D) instrumentation は「器楽編成法」の意味である。

覚えてトクする語彙

visual telephone 名 テレビ電話 ★★★
visually 副 見た目には、視覚的に ★★★
visualize 動 …を視覚化する、心に描く ★★★
visualization 名 視覚化、思い浮かべること ★★★
relevance 名 関連性、妥当性、適切さ (= relevancy) ★★★
irrelevant 形 関係のない、不適切な ★★★
irrelevance 名 不適切、的外れ (= irrelevancy) ★★★
purposeful 形 目的のある、意図をもった ★★★
purposeless 形 目的のない、無益な ★★★
purposely 副 わざと、故意に ★★★

解答・解説

Answer (C) 　　　　　　　　　　　　　　　　　　**Key Point** 品詞

スピーチをもっと効果的にするため、視覚資料はトピックと伝達目的にあったものにすべきである。

解法▶ make が「ある状態にする」という意味で用いられるとき、<make +目的語+補語>という文型をとる。スピーチを「効果的な」状態にするのだから、副詞ではなく形容詞の effective「効果的な」にする。

Chapter1　115

109

According to the press -------, they will close around 200 stores in 45 states as part of its restructuring.

(A) release
(B) released
(C) releasing
(D) to release

《語彙のヒント》

press 名 新聞、出版物 ★★★
[prés]
restructuring 名 リストラ ★★★
[rìːstrʌ́ktʃəriŋ]

110

Sara Willis Corp. will cut about 1,200 jobs as it scales back operations at three plants in Puerto Rico ------- produce underwear.

(A) which
(B) who
(C) where
(D) what

《語彙のヒント》

scale back ~ 熟 …をある割合で減じる、縮小する ★★★
[skéil bǽk]
underwear 名 下着 ★★★
[ʌ́ndərwèər]

第1章 ● パート5 短文穴埋め問題

覚えてトクする語彙

press clipping 名 新聞の切り抜き ★★★
press campaign 名 新聞によるキャンペーン ★★★
press agency 名 通信社（= news agency） ★★★
press conference 名 記者会見 ★★★
press briefing 名 報道陣向け説明会 ★★★
press kit 名 報道関係用配布資料 ★★★
restructure 動 …の構造を改革する ★★★
restructuring plan 名 （経営）再建策 ★★★
restructuring benefit 名 リストラ効果 ★★★
restructuring cost [charge] 名 リストラ費 ★★★

解答・解説

Answer (A) **Key Point** 品詞

新聞発表によると、彼らはリストラの1つとして、45の州の約200店舗を店じまいするとのことだ。

解法 → according to ～の to は前置詞なので、その後は名詞（句）にしなければならない。よって、press release「新聞発表、報道発表」と名詞形にする。

覚えてトクする語彙

scale up ～ 熟 …をある割合で増やす、拡大する ★★★
plant capacity 名 （工場の）生産能力 ★★★
plant manager 名 工場長 ★★★
Puerto Rican 形 プエルトリコの ★★★
undershirt 名 シャツ、肌着 ★★★
undershorts 名 《複数扱い》（男子・子供用の）パンツ、下着 ★★★
pants 名 《複数扱い、主にアメリカで》ズボン、スラックス ★★★
trousers 名 《複数扱い、主にイギリスで》ズボン ★★★

解答・解説

Answer (A) **Key Point** 関係詞

サラ・ウイリス社は、下着を製造するプエルトリコの3つの工場の操業を少しずつ縮小しているので、約1200の仕事を削除することになるだろう。

解法 → 先行詞は下着を製造している three plants「3つの工場」であり、人ではなく物なので、関係代名詞 which を用いる。もちろん、which の代わりに that を用いてもよい。

第2章

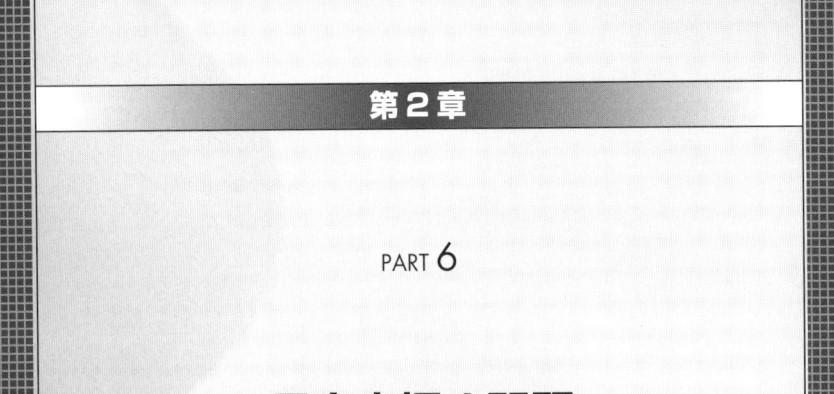

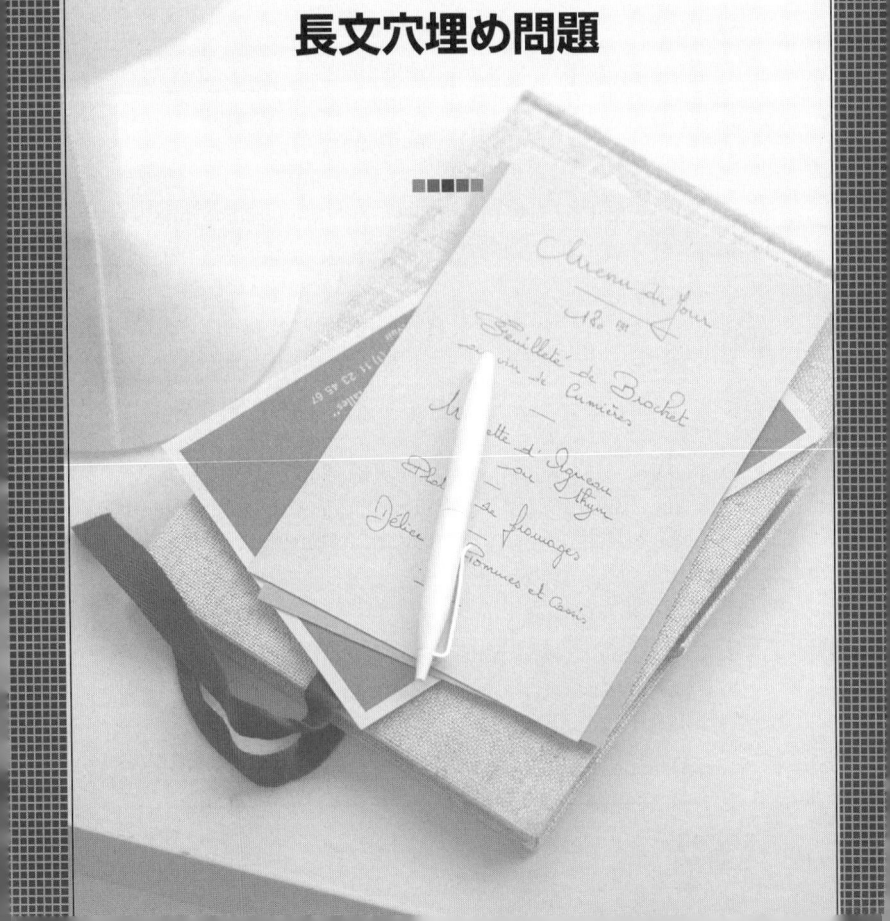

PART 6

長文穴埋め問題

001

Star Corporation is Iowa's most profitable business, in 2005 reporting $15 billion in sales. Since its _____ in 1928,

1. (A) founded
   (B) founding
   (C) finding
   (D) found

Star Corporation has developed more than 40,000 products. The company's goal is to _____ 30 percent of its sales

2. (A) enlarge
   (B) generate
   (C) operate
   (D) transact

from products that are less than 5 years old. Cellophane tape, masking tape and other adhesives still _____ a big part of

3. (A) make for
   (B) make out
   (C) make over
   (D) make up

the company's sales, but Star Corporation is also into electronic pain blockers used by dentists, fingerprint identification systems and other high-tech _____. Half of its business is

4. (A) devices
   (B) qualities
   (C) standards
   (D) orders

overseas. The company employs 18,000 people in Iowa.

《語彙のヒント》

profitable 形 もうかる、利益を生む ★★★
[práfitəbl]

billion 名 10億 ★★★
[bíljən]

masking tape 名 マスキングテープ、保護テープ ★★★
[mǽːskiŋ tèip]

adhesive 名 粘着テープ、接着剤 ★★★
[ədhíːsiv]

electronic 形 電子の ★★★
[ilektránik]

fingerprint 名 指紋 ★★★
[fíŋgərprìnt]

identification 名 鑑定、確認 ★★★
[aidèntifəkéiʃən]

high-tech 形 ハイテクの、最新式の ★★★
[háiték]

overseas 副 海外で、外国で ★★★
[òuvərsíːz]

日本語訳　　　　　　　　　　　　　　　　　　　　　　　　　　　translation

　スター・コーポレーションはアイオワ州で最も収益を上げている企業であり、2005年には売上高150億ドルを記録している。1928年創立以来、スター・コーポレーションは4万以上の製品を開発してきた。会社目標は商品となって5年に満たないもので、全売上高の30％を獲得することである。セロハンテープ、マスキングテープ、その他の粘着テープは今もなお会社の売上の大部分を占めているが、スター・コーポレーションは同時に歯科医の使用する電子式ペインブロッカーや指紋鑑定システム、その他の最新式機器も扱っている。ビジネスの半分は海外で行われている。同社はアイオワ州に1万8000人の従業員を擁している。

解答・解説　　　　　　　　　　　　　　　　　　　　　　　answer and explanation

Answer 1　　　　　　　　　　　　　　　　　　　　　　　　　　　　　　(B)
空欄の直前に its があるので、空欄には名詞が必要だとわかる。(B) と (C) が動名詞になっているが、意味から判断して (B) founding「設立、創立」が適切。

Answer 2　　　　　　　　　　　　　　　　　　　　　　　　　　　　　　(B)
会社目標は、商品となって5年に満たないもので全売上高の30％をどうすることかを考える。それぞれの選択肢の意味は、(A) enlarge「…を拡大する」、(B) generate「…を作り出す」、(C) operate「…を操作する」、(D) transact「…を取引する」である。空欄に適切なのは (B) のみである。

Answer 3　　　　　　　　　　　　　　　　　　　　　　　　　　　　　　(D)
セロハンテープ、マスキングテープ、その他の粘着テープが、会社の売上げの多くをどうしているのかを考える。ここは「…を占める、構成する」の意味を持つ熟語である (D) make up がぴったり合う。

Answer 4　　　　　　　　　　　　　　　　　　　　　　　　　　　　　　(A)
形容詞 high-tech「ハイテクの、最新の」に続く名詞として、文脈の中でどの語を入れるとよいかを考える。「ハイテク機器、最新機器」の意味にするのが妥当であろうから、(A) devices「機器」を選ぶ。

覚えてトクする語彙

profitability 名 収益性、利益率 ★★★
profitably 副 有利に、有効に ★★★
adhere 動 固執する、粘着する ★★★
adherent 形 執着する、粘着する ★★★
adhesive bandage 名 絆創膏 ★★★
electronics 名 電子工学 ★★★
fingertip 名 指先 ★★★
identifiable 形 身元を確認できる ★★★
oversee 動 …を監督する、監視する ★★★
overseer 名 監督者、職長 ★★★

MEMORANDUM

TO: All Office Employees
FROM: Roland Simeonson, President
RE: Appointment of Robert Sorley
DATE: September 25

Mr. Robert Sorley has _____ as the new manager of the

1. (A) appointed
   (B) to appoint
   (C) been appointed
   (D) been appointing

Operations Department here at Rexall Pharmaceuticals. He is _____ Dean Smith, who retired last week. This appointment

2. (A) replacing
   (B) substituting
   (C) converting
   (D) shifting

will become _____ October 1.

3. (A) effective
   (B) efficient
   (C) capable
   (D) competent

_____ this appointment, Mr. Sorley was the assistant manager

4. (A) Owing to
   (B) Prior to
   (C) According to
   (D) Thanks to

of the Operations Department at Northeastern Pharmaceuticals for the past 5 years.

　We will be having a reception to introduce Mr. Sorley this Friday at 6:00 p.m. We hope you will join us in the conference hall as we welcome him.

《語彙のヒント》

memorandum 名 社内回覧、メモ（= memo）　★★★
[mèmərǽndəm]

operations department 名 《the ～》営業部　★★★
[àpəréiʃənz dipáːrtmənt]

pharmaceutical 名 《～s》医薬品、薬事　★★★
[fɑ̀ːrməsúːtikəl]

reception 名 歓迎会、レセプション　★★★
[risépʃən]

conference hall 名 会議場　★★★
[kánfərəns hɔ́ːl]

日本語訳 　　　　　　　　　　　　　　　　　　　　　　　　　　　　　translation

社内回覧

宛先：　　全社員
差出人：　ローランド・シメオンソン社長
用件：　　ロバート・ソーリー氏の任命
差出日：　9月25日

　ロバート・ソーリー氏は、先週退職したディーン・スミス氏に代わって、レクソール製薬会社の営業部本部長に任命されました。この任命は 10 月 1 日より有効となります。
　この度の任命に先立って、ソーリー氏は過去5年間ノースイースタン製薬会社の営業部副部長を務めてこられました。
　今週金曜日午後6時よりソーリー氏を全従業員に紹介するための歓迎会を開きます。皆様には会議ホールにご参集いただき、一緒に氏を歓迎して頂ければと願います。

解答・解説 　　　　　　　　　　　　　　　　　　　　　　　answer and explanation

Answer 1. 　　　　　　　　　　　　　　　　　　　　　　　　　　　　　　　(C)
RE:「…について」の部分を見ると、Robert Sorley 氏が任命されたということがわかる。よって、空欄の部分には「任命された」という受動態を入れる必要がある。よって、(C) が正解となる。

Answer 2. 　　　　　　　　　　　　　　　　　　　　　　　　　　　　　　　(A)
Dean Smith 氏の退職に伴い、Robert Sorley 氏が営業部の新しい部長となるわけだから、空欄には「…に取って代わる、…の跡を継ぐ」の意味を持つ replace の進行形（未来の予定を表している）の (A) を入れる。(B) の substituting の場合は、substituting for であれば問題ない。

Answer 3. 　　　　　　　　　　　　　　　　　　　　　　　　　　　　　　　(A)
空欄の後には日付が来ている。よって、ここは「(…より、…から) 効力を生じて、有効で」の意味を表す (A) effective が正解となる。

Answer 4. 　　　　　　　　　　　　　　　　　　　　　　　　　　　　　　　(B)
空欄の後は、Sorely 氏のこれまでの経歴について述べている。従って、空欄には「この度の任命以前は」という意味になるはずなので、prior to「…より先に」(= before) を入れるとよい。他の選択肢の意味は、(A) owing to「…せいで」、(C) according to「…によれば」、(D) thanks to「…のおかげで」である。

覚えてトクする語彙

pharmacist 名 薬剤師 ★★★
pharmacy 名 薬局、薬学 ★★★
reception desk 名 フロント、受付 ★★★
wedding reception 名 結婚披露宴 ★★★
receptionist 名 受付係 ★★★
conference call 名 電話会議、会議通話 ★★★

Software Unlimited

2127 Van Buren Street, Palm Bay, FL 32907-4489

Mr. Henry Nelson
36 Schooner Ridge Rd.
Cumberland Foreside, ME 04110

Dear Mr. Nelson:

We have received your letter of February 20 to the _____ that

1. (A) effect
　(B) fact
　(C) conclusion
　(D) report

the CD-ROM SX-420 you ordered has not yet arrived. Upon checking our records, we are very sorry to inform you that this product has been sold out and that we failed to inform you that we were unable to _____ your order. In its place we are now selling a similar

2. (A) fulfill
　(B) arrange
　(C) establish
　(D) draw

product, CD-ROM SX-560. This is the newest model and the price is $40 more than the model you ordered. Due to the trouble we have caused you, we would like to offer you the new model at the same price as the old one.

Please notify us if you would like to go ahead and receive the new model or not. If you would like the new model, we will ship it to you immediately. If not, we will promptly _____ the $350 you have

3. (A) recover
   (B) refund
   (C) redeem
   (D) reimburse

sent along with your order for product SX-420.

Again, we apologize for your inconvenience and appreciate your patience. We hope that this arrangement will be _____ to you.

4. (A) contented
   (B) comprehensive
   (C) satisfactory
   (D) delightful

Sincerely,

Lois Anderson

Lois Anderson
Customer Service Supervisor

語彙のヒント

model 名 型、デザイン、モデル ★★★
[mádl]

due to ～ 熟 …のために、…の原因で（= owing to, because of） ★★★
[djúː tu]

notify 動 …に知らせる ★★★
[nóutəfài]

go ahead 熟 押し進める、始める ★★★
[góu əhéd]

ship 動 …を出荷する、運送する ★★★
[ʃíp]

promptly 副 迅速に、即刻 ★★★
[prámptli]

apologize 動 謝罪する、謝る ★★★
[əpálədʒàiz]

inconvenience 名 迷惑、不便、不都合 ★★★
[ìnkənvíːnjəns]

arrangement 名 手配、手はず ★★★
[əréindʒmənt]

customer service 名 顧客サービス部門 ★★★
[kástəmər sə́ːrvis]

supervisor 名 主任、管理者 ★★★
[súːpərvàizər]

日本語訳 — translation

ソフトウェア・アンリミッティッド
2127 ヴァン・ブーレン通り、パーム・ベイ、フロリダ州 32907-4489

ヘンリー・ネルソン様
36 スクーナー・リッジ・ロード
カンバーランド・フォーサイド、メイン州 04110

ネルソン様

　弊社はお客様のご注文なさいました CD-ROM SX-420 がまだ届いていないという旨の2月20日付のお手紙を受け取りました。弊社の記録を確認しましたところ、大変申し訳ございませんが、本商品はすでに売り切れておりまして、弊社はお客様の注文に応じることはできないという通知を怠っておりました。その商品の代わりに、弊社では現在 CD-ROM SX-560 という類似品を販売しております。これは最新モデルであり、お客様がご注文なさいましたモデルよりも40ドル高いものです。ご迷惑をおかけしたお詫びとしまして、弊社ではお客様に新型モデルを旧型モデルと同じ値段でご提供したいと考えております。

　その対応措置に賛同し、新型モデルを受け取りたいかどうかを弊社までご連絡下さい。新型モデルを希望なさる場合には、至急発送致します。そうでない場合には、SX-420をご注文なさいました際にお送り頂きました３５０ドルを早急に払い戻しさせて頂きます。

　繰り返しになりますが、お客様にご迷惑をおかけして誠に申し訳ございません

でした。もうしばらくお待ち下さいますようお願い申し上げます。この度の措置がお客様に満足頂けるものになればと思う次第です。

敬具
ロイス・アンダーソン
顧客サービス部門主任

解答・解説

Answer 1. (A)
空欄の後が that 節になっていることから、ここは to the effect that ~「…という旨の」にするのが正しい。この to the effect that ~の部分は空欄前の your letter of February 20 を後位から修飾している。

Answer 2. (A)
文脈からこの会社は顧客の注文を履行することができなかったということが分かる。よって、fulfill your order「貴方の注文(品)を満たす、履行する、調達する」が正解となる。

Answer 3. (B)
もしも顧客が会社としての対応措置が気に入らない場合には、すでに顧客が支払っている 350 ドルを会社はどうするかを考える。当然、その代金は払い戻しするであろうから、pay back の意味を持つ (B) refund「…を払い戻す」を選ぶのが適切となる。他の選択肢の意味は、(A) recover「…を回収する、取り戻す」、(C) redeem「…を買い戻す、弁済する」、(D) reimburse「(借りたお金)を返済する、償還する」である。

Answer 4. (C)
この度の措置が顧客に対してどのようなものであって欲しいと会社が望むかを考える。適切なのは、(C) satisfactory「満足のゆく」のみである。(D) delightful は「愉快な、とても楽しい」の意味である。

覚えてトクする語彙

model agency 名 モデル事務所 ★★★
notifiable 形 届け出る義務のある ★★★
notification 名 通知、告知、届け出 ★★★
shipment 名 出荷、貨物、船荷 ★★★
shipping 名 船積み、運送業 ★★★
prompt 形 即座の、機敏な 動 …を刺激する ★★★
apology 名 謝罪、詫び ★★★
inconvenient 形 不便な、迷惑な ★★★
arranged marriage 名 見合い結婚 ★★★
supervise 動 …を監督する、管理する、指揮する ★★★
supervision 名 監督、管理 ★★★
supervisory 形 監督の、管理上の ★★★

BUSINESS OPPORTUNITIES

Secretary / Receptionist

We are a company on the move. K.T. & Associates, Inc. is an
_____ marketing and sales firm based in Minnesota. One

1. (A) establish
   (B) establishing
   (C) established
   (D) establishment

of the offices located in Minneapolis is now _____

2. (A) asking
   (B) seeking
   (C) demanding
   (D) appealing

an individual who is a self-starter, well organized,
with good communication skills. Duties _____ general

3. (A) imply
   (B) include
   (C) enter
   (D) claim

office responsibilities, answering and directing phone calls and
data entry. Should be comfortable with Microsoft Word and
Excel.

_____ person with excellent attendance record. Position

4. (A) depending
   (B) dependence
   (C) dependent
   (D) dependable

will be available from September 1st. Flexible schedule, 20-30 hrs per week. Résumé with cover letter should be sent to:

> K.T.& Associates, Inc.
> 245 Cedar Ave.
> Minneapolis, MN 55402
> ATTN: Human Resources

Phone, fax, and e-mail applications will not be processed.

《語彙のヒント》

receptionist 名 受付係 ★★★
[risépʃənist]

on the move 熟 発展中の、活気のある ★★★
[ən ðə múːv]

self-starter 名 自発的に物事をやる人 ★★★
[sélfstáːrtər]

duty 名 任務、責務、義務 ★★★
[djúːti]

entry 名 入力 ★★★
[éntri]

flexible 形 フレックス制の、融通の利く、柔軟な ★★★
[fléksəbl]

hrs 名 時間（hours の省略形） ★★★
[áuərz]

résumé 名 履歴書 ★★★
[rézuméi]

ATTN 名 …宛て（attention の省略形） ★★★
[əténʃən]

human resources 名 人事部 ★★★
[hjúːmən risɔ́ːrsiz]

process 動 …を処理する、扱う 名 過程、加工 ★★★
[práses]

日本語訳

ビジネス・チャンス

秘書／受付係

弊社は活気ある発展中の会社です。K.T.& Associates 社はミネソタに基盤を置く定評あるマーケティング兼セールス会社です。ミネアポリスにあるオフィスの1つが現在、自発的に行動ができ、きちんと整理ができ、優れたコミュニケーション能力を有する人を探しています。職務内容は、一般的なオフィス業務、電話の応答と案内、データ入力を含みます。マイクロソフト・ワードとエクセルを楽に操作できなければなりません。信頼できる精勤者を望みます。ポジションは9月1日から可能となります。フレックスタイム制で、週20〜30時間の労働です。履歴書はカバーレターを添えて以下へご郵送下さい。

K.T.& Associates 社
245 シーダー・アベニュー
ミネアポリス、ミネソタ州　55402
人事部宛て

電話、ファックス、電子メールでの応募申し込みは受付致しません。

解答・解説

Answer 1. (C)
どのような marketing and sales firm であるかを考えて、適切な形容詞を空欄に入れる。正解は（C）established「定評のある、確立した」である。

Answer 2. (B)
この会社は空欄の後に述べられているような人材をどうしたいのかを考える。この求人広告全体を見てもわかる通り、会社はそのような人材を募集しているわけである。よって、seek「…を探す、捜し求める」の進行形である（B）が正解となる。

Answer 3. (B)
空欄には、duties「任務、職務内容」はいくつかの事務職を「含む」という動詞が入るとよい。よって、(B) include が正解である。

Answer 4. (D)
それぞれの選択肢の意味は(A) depending「頼って、依存して」(動詞 depend の~ing形)、(B) dependence「依頼、依存」、(C) dependent「頼っている」、(D) dependable「信頼できる、頼みになる」である。精勤者を求めているわけなので、信頼できる人物でなければならない。よって、(D) dependable が正解となる。

覚えてトクする語彙

reception clerk 名 (ホテルの) フロント係 ★★★
reception desk 名 フロント、受付 ★★★
entry fee 名 入場料 ★★★
entry visa 名 入国ビザ ★★★
entryway 名 入り口用通路 ★★★
dependability 名 信頼性 ★★★
flexibility 名 柔軟性、融通性 ★★★
flextime 名 フレックスタイム、自由勤務時間制 ★★★
resume 動 …を再開する、取り戻す ★★★
human resources development 名 人材開発、能力開発 ★★★
application deadline 名 願書締切 ★★★
processed 形 加工された ★★★
processed food 名 加工食品 ★★★

Johnson Steel Corporation

J S C

1113 South 14th Street
Montgomery, Alabama 78872-8332
Telephone (808) 398-2132
Fax (808) 398-2236

May 27

Mr. Tim Benedict
Box 283
Auburn, Alabama 78341-7319

Dear Mr. Benedict:

We _____ to inform you that for the job of sales

1. (A) deny
   (B) miss
   (C) regret
   (D) neglect

representative we have hired another applicant who
_____ meets our current needs. We have carefully

2. (A) very
   (B) much
   (C) more
   (D) better

checked your credentials. As a result, we have decided that we need someone with more outside sales experience in a business-to-business environment.

You have greatly impressed us, however, with your potential, your desire to succeed in business and your strong communication skills.

We hope, therefore, that you will apply _____ a position

3. (A) to
   (B) in
   (C) for
   (D) with

with our company at some time in the future. We would like to hear from you again after you have gained more on-the-job experience.

We would like to thank you for considering our company. We wish you the best of luck in your job _____ efforts.

4. (A) land
   (B) search
   (C) procure
   (D) research

Very truly yours,

James Carrico

James Carrico
Director of Personnel

《語彙のヒント》

steel 名 鉄鋼 ★★★
[stíːl]

sales representative 名 販売員 ★★★
[séilz reprizèntətiv]

credential 名 経歴、資格、適性 ★★★
[kridénʃəl]

as a result 熟 結果として ★★★
[əz ə rizʌ́lt]

business-to-business 形 企業間の、ビジネス間の ★★★
[bíznəstəbíznəs]

impress 動 …に強い印象を与える、…を感動させる ★★★
[imprés]

potential 名 潜在能力、可能性 ★★★
[pəténʃəl]

on-the-job 名 実地の、職場の ★★★
[ənðədʒɑ́b]

consider 動 …を考慮する、考えてみる ★★★
[kənsídər]

personnel 名 人事課、人材、職員 ★★★
[pə̀ːrsənél]

日本語訳

ジョンソン鉄鋼会社
1113 サウス14番通り
モンゴメリー、アラバマ州 78872-8332
電話 (808) 398-2132
ファクス (808) 398-2236

5月27日

ティム・ベネディクト様
私書箱283
オーバーン、アラバマ州 78341-7319

ベネディクト様:

　誠に申し訳ございませんが、営業担当の職に対して、弊社の現在のニーズにより合う別の応募者を採用することに致しました。弊社は貴殿の経歴・資格を慎重に判定いたしました。結果として、弊社は企業間環境の中で営業の実地経験のより豊かな人が必要であると判断致しました。

　しかしながら、私どもは貴殿の潜在能力、ビジネスにおける成功願望、優れたコミュニケーション能力に非常に感銘を受けました。従いまして、貴殿にはいつか近いうちに弊社のポジションに応募して頂ければと思う次第です。さらなる実地経験を積まれた後に、またご連絡頂きたく存じます。

この度は弊社をご検討頂きまして心より感謝申し上げます。貴殿の就職活動がうまくいくことをお祈り致します。

敬具
ジェームズ・キャリコ
人事部長

解答・解説

Answer 1. (C)
この手紙文全体を読むと、この手紙の目的は求人の応募者に不採用の通知をすることであることがわかる。よって、「残念ながら…する」の意味を表す regret to do を用いるのが適切である。

Answer 2. (D)
会社は Benedict 氏よりも職務・仕事を遂行する資質、能力がさらに高い別の応募者を採用することに決めたのである。よって、その人の方が会社の現行のニーズに合うわけだから、who better meets our current needs. とするのが正しい。

Answer 3. (C)
(A) か (C) か迷う人が多い。apply to ～は直後に場所が、apply for ～は直後に事・物が来る。ここでは、直後に a position が来ているので、(C) apply for が正解となる。

Answer 4. (B)
空欄の前後の意味を考えて、ここは job search「仕事探し、就職活動」にするのが正しい。空欄には名詞が入るべきであるし、意味的に考えても、(B) 以外の選択肢は当てはまらない。

覚えてトクする語彙

steelworker [名] 製鉄所の工員 ★★★
steely [形] 堅固な、冷酷な ★★★
credence [名] 信用、信頼 ★★★
result in ～ [熟] …という結果に終わる ★★★
result from ～ [熟] …から結果として起きる ★★★
impression [名] 印象、感銘 ★★★
impressive [形] 深い感銘を与える、印象的である ★★★
potency [名] 影響力、威力、効果 ★★★
potent [形] 強い効果を持つ、強力な ★★★
potentially [副] 可能性として、ひょっとすると ★★★
considerate [形] 思いやりのある、優しい ★★★
considerable [形] かなりの、相当の ★★★
consideration [名] 熟慮、考慮、思いやり、配慮 ★★★
considering [前] …を考慮すれば ★★★

第3章

PART 7

読解問題

1つの文書
2つの文書

Questions 1-2 refer to the following instructions.

> Instructions for Completing the New Business Tax Registration Form
>
> 1) Fill in your name and any alias.
> 2) Complete your business name and address. Do not use a post office box, use a street address.
> 3) Enter your business telephone number. Fill in your contact telephone number if different form your business telephone number.
> 4) If applicable, write in your business license number and expiration date.
> 5) Choose and enter your registration fee amount corresponding to your type of business.
> 6) Estimate and fill in your tax for the coming year.
> 7) If delinquent for last year, enter the penalty tax amount, calculate the interest on your penalty tax and fill in the total amount due.
> 8) Enter the amount of payment you are enclosing in this form. This is essential to process your form.
> 9) Specify payment method: credit card, money order or check. Please print credit card numbers clearly and sign on the signature line for authorization.
> 10) Specify your business activity. This is necessary to classify your business correctly.
> 11) Remit your payment along with your New Business Tax Registration Form to the address on page 1.
>
> Complete ALL questions, as incomplete forms cannot be processed. Enclose payment with this form otherwise the form cannot be processed. If you have any questions please contact our free-phone help line on 0800-677-323 during office hours.

第3章 ● パート7 読解問題（1つの文書）

Q1　Why is it necessary to state the type of business you do?
　　(A) So they can process your credit card correctly.
　　(B) So they can assign your business to the right group.
　　(C) So they can assess the correct payment method.
　　(D) So they can estimate your delinquent tax for the previous year.

Q2　What will happen if payment is not enclosed?
　　(A) The form cannot be processed.
　　(B) The form will be processed with a small delay.
　　(C) The form will be sent back to you.
　　(D) You should wait to be contacted.

語彙のヒント

alias 图 別名、通称　★★★
[éiliəs]
post office box 图 私書箱（= P.O. Box, POB）　★★★
[póust ɔ́:fis bɑ̀ks]
applicable 形 適用できる　★★★
[ǽplikəbl]
expiration 图 終了、満期（= ending）　★★★
[èkspəréiʃən]
corresponding 形 対応する、一致する　★★★
[kɔ̀:rəspándiŋ]
delinquent 形 （負債・税金などが）滞納の、支払期限を過ぎた、義務を怠る　★★★
[dilíŋkwənt]
remit 動 （金銭）を（郵便などで）送る　★★★
[rimít]

日本語訳

質問1～2は、次の記入説明書に関するものです。

新事業税金登録用紙記入のための説明

1) 名前と通称を記入してください。
2) 事業名と住所をお書きください。私書箱は使わず、番地をお書きください。
3) 事業所電話番号を記入してください。事業所電話番号と異なる番号に連絡がほしい場合はその番号をお書きください。
4) 適用があれば、事業免許番号とその期限をお書きください。
5) 事業種と対応する登録費を選び、記入してください。
6) 次年度の税金を見積もりご記入ください。
7) 昨年度滞納の場合は、罰金税額を記入し、罰金税額の利子を計算し、総額をお書きください。
8) この用紙と同封する支払額を記入してください。書類を処理するのに不可欠です。
9) クレジットカード・郵便為替・小切手など、支払方法をお選びください。クレジットカード番号ははっきりとお書きください。承認のため署名欄にサインしてください。
10) 事業活動を特定してください。事業を正確に分類するのに必要です。
11) 1ページの住所に、新事業税金登録用紙とともに、支払額を送金してください。

不完全な書類は処理できませんので、すべての事項を完全にしてください。この用紙とともに支払いをお送りいただけないと、お取り扱いできません。ご質問があれば、フリーダイヤル 0800-677-323 まで営業時間中にお電話ください。

Q1 事業の種類を言う必要があるのはなぜですか。
 (A) クレジットカードを正確に処理できるから。
 (B) 事業を正しいグループに割り当てられるから。
 (C) 正しい支払い方法にアクセスできるから。
 (D) 昨年度の滞納税金額を見積もることができるから。

Q2 支払いが同封されていないと、どうなりますか。
 (A) 書類は処理されない。
 (B) 書類の処理が少し遅れる。
 (C) 書類は送り返される。
 (D) 連絡があるまで待つ。

第3章 ● パート7 読解問題（1つの文書）

解答・解説 — answer and explanation

Answer 1　　　　　　　　　　　　　　　　　　　　　　　　　　　　　　(B)
10) Specify your business activity. This is necessary to classify your business correctly. とあるので、(B) を選ぶ。

Answer 2　　　　　　　　　　　　　　　　　　　　　　　　　　　　　　(A)
最後の段落に Enclose payment with this form otherwise the form cannot be processed. とあるので、正解は、(A) である。

覚えてトクする語彙

box number [名] 私書箱番号　★★★
expire [動] 期限が切れて無効となる、(契約などが) 終了する、満期になる　★★★
correspond [動] 一致する、調和する、文通する《with, to》　★★★
correspondent [名] 文通する人、記者、対応するもの　★★★
correspondence [名] 一致すること、文通、通信　★★★
delinquency [名] (職務などの) 怠慢・不履行、犯罪、非行　★★★
juvenile delinquency [名] 少年非行　★★★
remittance [名] 送金額、送金すること　★★★
remission [名] (負債・罰金・税金などの) 免除 (= remittal)　★★★
remissible [形] (罪・罰金などが) 許される、免じられる　★★★

Questions 1-2 refer to the following form.

Print and complete this form for mail orders. Prices & discount offers are guaranteed for 1 week from the date this form is downloaded.

ID	Product	Price Each	Quantity
MNM	**Meles New Movie 1**	**$30**	**1**
AM2	**Ants Movie 2**	**$25**	**1**
ST	**Sports Today**	**$20**	**2**

Shipping: $5.00 PER ITEM

PAYMENT OPTIONS

Enclose a Bank Check or Money Order in US Dollars for the amount due. You may also pay by printing and filling out the credit card form below. Do not send personal checks. In most countries, you can buy a Money Order at the Post Office for an amount in US Dollars, and most banks will be able to issue a check in US Dollars for you. Refunds are only available if the DVDs received are found to be faulty.

Q1 Which payment option is NOT acceptable to pay for the mail order
    DVDs?
    (A) Bank check
    (B) Money order
    (C) Personal check
    (D) Credit card

Q2 How much will the total cost be for the DVDs shown in the form above?
    (A) $75
    (B) $95
    (C) $110
    (D) $115

《語彙のヒント》

mail order 名 通信注文（販売）　★★★
[méil ɔ́ːrdər]
download 動 …をダウンロードする、データを自分のコンピュータに取り込む　★★★
[dáunlòud]
money order 名 （郵便）為替　★★★
[mʌ́ni ɔ́ːrdər]
faulty 形 欠点のある、不完全な　★★★
[fɔ́ːlti]

日本語訳

質問1〜2は、次の申し込み用紙に関するものです。

通信販売のご注文は、この用紙を印刷・ご記入の上郵送してください。価格と値引きは、この用紙がダウンロードされた日から1週間の間保証されます。

品番	製品	価格	量
MNM	Meles New Movie 1	30ドル	1
AM2	Ants Movie 2	25ドル	1
ST	Sports Today	20ドル	2

送料：1商品につき5ドル

お支払い方法
アメリカドルで総額分の銀行小切手か郵便為替を同封してください。または、下のクレジットカード用の書類にご記入の上、クレジットカードでお支払いいただくこともできます。個人用小切手は送らないでください。ほとんどの国では、郵便局でアメリカドルの郵便為替を購入できますし、銀行でアメリカドルの小切手をお求めいただけます。お届けのDVDに欠陥がある場合のみ、払い戻しをいたします。

Q1 DVDを注文の際、不可能な支払い方法はどれですか。
 (A) 銀行小切手
 (B) 郵便為替
 (C) 個人小切手
 (D) クレジットカード

Q2 上の注文書に書かれているDVDの総額はいくらになりますか。
 (A) 75ドル
 (B) 95ドル
 (C) 110ドル
 (D) 115ドル

第3章 ● パート7 読解問題（1つの文書）

解答・解説 — *answer and explanation*

Answer 1 (C)

「お支払い方法」のところに Do not send personal checks. とあるので（C）が正解となる。

Answer 2 (D)

商品の代金が 95 ドル（Meles New Movie 1 $30 + Ants Movie 2 $25 + Sports Today $20 × 2）で、DVD4本分の送料が 20 ドル（$5 × 4）だから、合計で（D）115 ドルになる。

覚えてトクする語彙

mail-order house 名 通信販売会社（= mail-order company） ★★★
mail box 名 ポスト、（個人の）郵便受け ★★★
mailing address 名 郵送先 ★★★
upload 動 …をアップロードする、情報をネットワークにのせる ★★★
fault 名 欠点、欠陥 ★★★
faultless 形 欠点のない ★★★
fault finding 名 あら探し ★★★

Questions 1-2 refer to the following advertisement.

Sometimes it seems your seasonal allergies want to make you miserable in as many ways as they can. That's when you need the multi-symptom relief of Polleglin. Polleglin is specifically designed to block the histamine that triggers allergic responses like runny nose, itchy eyes and scratchy throat, which may be one reason it's the number one prescription antihistamine. Polleglin is for people 12 and older. Side effects are low and may include headache, cold or back pain. Talk to your doctor about Polleglin.

Polleglin. So Much Relief for So Many Symptoms.

For more information call 1-800-polleglin. Join the extras program @ polleglin.com.

Q1 What symptom is Polleglin NOT effective for?
   (A) Scratchy eyes
   (B) Tickling throat
   (C) Nose bleeding
   (D) Allergic reactions

Q2 Which side effect may Polleglin cause?
   (A) Heartache
   (B) Toothache
   (C) Stomachache
   (D) Backache

第3章 ● パート7 読解問題（1つの文書）

《語彙のヒント》

seasonal 形 季節的な、ある季節に限った ★★★
[síːzənl]

allergy 名 アレルギー ★★★
[ǽlərdʒi]

miserable 形 みじめな、不幸な ★★★
[mízərəbl]

multi-symptom 名 さまざまな症状 ★★★
[mÀltisímptəm]

block 動 …をふさぐ、閉鎖する ★★★
[blák]

histamine 名 ヒスタミン（たんぱく質の分解による有毒成分。体内にたまるとアレルギー症状が起こるといわれる） ★★★
[hístəmìːn]

trigger 動 …を起こす、誘発する ★★★
[trígər]

itchy 形 かゆい、むずがゆい ★★★
[ítʃi]

scratchy 形 ちくちくする、かゆい ★★★
[skrǽtʃi]

side effect 名 副作用 ★★★
[sáid ifèkt]

tickle 動 むずむずする、ちくちくする ★★★
[tíkl]

nose bleeding 名 鼻血 ★★★
[nóuz blìːdiŋ]

reaction 名 反応 ★★★
[riǽkʃən]

■ 日本語訳

質問1～2は、次の広告に関するものです。

アレルギーをお持ちの方は、その季節が来ると、いろいろな症状が出て、たいへんつらいものです。そんなとき、諸症状を抑えるポレグリンをお使いください。ポレグリンは、鼻水・目のかゆみ・のどのいがいがなどアレルギーの諸症状を引き起こすヒスタミンをブロックするので、処方されている抗ヒスタミン剤で、最も人気があります。ポレグリンは、12歳以上の方が服用できます。副作用はあまりありませんが、頭痛・風邪・腰痛を伴うことがあります。ポレグリンに関しては専門医にご相談ください。

ポレグリン　諸症状がずっと楽になります

さらなる情報が必要な方は、1-800-polleglin へお電話ください。おまけのプログラム polleglin.com. にもご参加ください。

Q1 ポレグリンが効果的でない症状はどれですか。
　(A) 目のかゆみ
　(B) のどの痛み
　(C) 鼻血
　(D) アレルギー反応

Q2 ポレグリンが引き起こすかもしれない副作用はどれですか。
　(A) 胸痛
　(B) 歯痛
　(C) 腹痛
　(D) 腰痛

第3章 ● パート7 読解問題（1つの文書）

解答・解説　　　　　　　　　　　　　　　　　　　　　　　answer and explanation

Answer 1　　　　　　　　　　　　　　　　　　　　　　　　　　　　　　　(C)
3文目の後半に that triggers allergic responses like runny nose, itchy eyes and scratchy throat. とあるので、書かれていないのは、(C) の Nose bleeding「鼻血」だとわかる。

Answer 2　　　　　　　　　　　　　　　　　　　　　　　　　　　　　　　(D)
5文目に、include headache, cold or back pain とあり、back pain のみが書かれているので、(D) Backache「腰痛」を選ぶ。

覚えてトクする語彙

seasonable [形] 季節にふさわしい、時節柄の　★★★
allergic [形] アレルギーの　★★★
allergen [名] アレルギー抗体　★★★
allergist [名] アレルギー専門医　★★★
misery [名] 悲惨、みじめさ　★★★
symptom [名] 症状　★★★
blockade [名] （進行・交通の）障害（物）、（氷雪などによる）不通　★★★
antihistamine [名] 抗ヒスタミン　★★★
react [動] 反応する《to》　★★★
reactionary [形] 反動の、反作用の、逆戻りの　★★★

Questions 1-3 refer to the following letter.

John Jones
12 South Street
Brisbane
Queensland

April 12, 2006

Mr. Richard S. Smith
Pharmaceuticals, Ltd.
23 James Street
Sydney

Dear Mr. Smith,

Thank you for your interview yesterday. I found it most interesting and I enjoyed meeting you and your office staff.

After leaving your office, I thought of a point I would like to add to our conversation. I believe that by doing more consumer research, we might find out how to improve sales.

Of course, this would increase the cost which is often a deterrent to such an approach. However, as discussed yesterday, the company needs to find what people really think about our products as is the case throughout the whole pharmaceutical industry. Detailed consumer research concerning each product would be the best way to establish which products need improvement.

For example, we have no accurate data on consumer reaction to our new offer of over-the-counter, generic drugs. If we are to increase profits in the future, we need a well focused, consumer research plan, and this should be implemented as soon as possible. With your approval, I would like to draw up such a plan for my proposal including a detailed budget.

In a few days, I will follow up these ideas on the telephone. Thank you again for the interview.

Sincerely yours,

John Jones

John Jones

Q1 What is the purpose of this letter?
(A) To say thank you for the interview
(B) To arrange another meeting
(C) To talk about the disadvantages of consumer research
(D) To suggest a way to improve sales for the company

Q2 What does the writer John Jones suggest they do?
(A) Make a detailed plan for the next budget
(B) Get accurate date about future profits
(C) Find out about consumer attitudes to their products
(D) Gain approval for their new over-the-counter generic drugs

Q3 What is the writer going to do after sending this letter?
(A) Start doing consumer research
(B) Contact Mr. Smith about the proposal
(C) Talk to staff and thank them for the interview
(D) Wait for Mr. Smith to telephone him later

《語彙のヒント》

Ltd. 名 有限会社（= limited company） ★★★
[límitid]

deterrent 形 妨げる、抑止する ★★★
[ditə́:rənt]

accurate 形 正確な ★★★
[ǽkjurət]

over-the-counter 形 処方箋のいらない、一般市販薬の ★★★
[óuvərðəkáuntər]

generic 形 （薬などが）一般名称で販売される、ノーブランドの ★★★
[dʒənérik]

approval 名 承認、正式な認可 ★★★
[əprú:vəl]

draw up ~ 熟 …を作成する ★★★
[drɔ́: ʌp]

proposal 名 企画、提案 ★★★
[prəpóuzəl]

follow up ~ 熟 …をさらに徹底させる、引き続いて…する ★★★
[fálou ʌp]

■ 日本語訳　　　　　　　　　　　　　　　　　　　　　　　　　　　　translation

質問1～3は次の手紙に関するものです。

ジョン・ジョーンズ
南通り12番地
ブリスベン
クイーンランド

2006年4月12日

リチャード・S・スミス様
Pharmaceuticals 社
ジェイムス通り23番地
シドニー

スミス様
昨日はお世話になりありがとうございました。会談は興味深く、スミス氏をはじ

めオフィスの皆様にお目にかかれ光栄でした。

会談終了後、ひとつ言い忘れたことがあるのに気づきました。それは、顧客調査をもっと行うことで販売が改善できるということです。

もちろん、これはコストがかかり、それがしばしばさまたげとなっていることと思います。しかしながら、昨日お話しましたように、製薬産業全体に言えることですが、会社は自社製品について人々がどう思っているかを知ることが必要です。それぞれの製品について詳しい顧客調査をすることは、どの製品に改善の余地があるかを立証する最善策でしょう。

例えば、貴社の処方箋なしで購入できる一般名称で販売される薬品の新企画には、正確な顧客の反応データがありません。将来利益を増やしたいのなら、焦点を定めた顧客調査計画が必要で、できるだけ早くこれを実行しなければなりません。

ご承認いただけましたら、詳細な予算を含んだ提案書を作成したく思います。

数日のうちに、このプランをさらに徹底させるため、お電話をさしあげたいと思います。会談の機会をご提供くださりありがとうございました。

敬具

ジョン・ジョーンズ

Q1 この手紙の目的は何ですか。
　(A) 会談のお礼を言うため
　(B) 次の会合を設定するため
　(C) 顧客調査のデメリットを話すため
　(D) 会社の売上改善の方法を提案するため

Q2 この手紙を書いたジョン・ジョーンズは何を提案していますか。
　(A) 次の予算の詳細な計画を作成する
　(B) 将来の収益について正確なデータを得る
　(C) 会社の製品に対する顧客の態度を探る
　(D) 処方箋なしで購入できる一般名称で販売される薬品の承認を得る

Q3 この手紙を送った後、手紙の差出人はどうするつもりですか。
(A) 顧客調査を始める
(B) 提案についてスミス氏に連絡を取る
(C) 職員と話し会談のお礼を言う
(D) スミス氏からの電話を待つ

解答・解説　answer and explanation

Answer 1 (D)
第2段落に I believe that by doing more consumer research, we might find out how to improve sales. とあり、第3段落以下販売改善について書かれているので、(D) が正解となる。

Answer 2 (C)
第2段落の I believe that by doing more consumer research, we might find out how to improve sales. と第3段落の the company needs to find what people really think about our products から、顧客調査を提案していることがわかるので、正解は (C) となる。

Answer 3 (B)
最後の段落に In a few days, I will follow up these ideas on the telephone. とあるので、ジョーンズの方から電話をするということがわかり、(B) が正解となる。

覚えてトクする語彙

deterrence 名 抑止、妨害 ★★★
accuracy 名 正確さ ★★★
approve 動 …を是認する、認可する ★★★
approvable 形 是認できる、推賞できる ★★★
approved 形 認可されている、公認の ★★★
approving 形 是認する、賛成する ★★★
approver 名 賛同者 ★★★
draw on ～ 熟 …を利用する、活用する ★★★
draw near 熟 近づく ★★★
draw a blank 熟 思い出せない ★★★
draw the curtain over [on] ～ 熟 …を秘密にしておく ★★★
propose 動 …を提案する ★★★
follow *one's* nose 熟 人の例にならう ★★★
follow in *a person's* footsteps 熟 まっすぐに進む、直感に頼る ★★★
follow suit to ～ 熟 …の例にならう ★★★

Questions 1-2 refer to the following news article.

> SEOUL --- South Korea's current account surplus fell to 1.17 billion dollars last month, down sharply from 2.03 billion dollars a year earlier, the central Bank to Korea said Tuesday.
>
>   The current account is a broad measure of trade in merchandise and services.
>
>   The current account surplus during the first 10 months of this year fell to 8.65 billion dollars from 20.83 billion dollars in the same period last year, the central bank said.
>
>   The trade surplus fell to a surplus of 1.53 billion dollars last month, from a surplus of 2.62 billion dollars a year earlier because of growing imports and slowing export growths.
>
>   Customs-cleared imports rose 24.1 percent in October while exports rose only 14.7 percent.

Q1 How much was the trade surplus last month?
- (A) 1.17 billion dollars
- (B) 1.53 billion dollars
- (C) 2.03 billion dollars
- (D) 2.62 billion dollars

Q2 What can be inferred from the article?
- (A) Exports this year are growing more than last year.
- (B) The current account is the most important economic indicator.
- (C) The economy last year was better than this year.
- (D) The economy in South Korea is improving this year.

《語彙のヒント》

current account 名 当座預金 ★★★
[kə́:rənt əkáunt]

surplus 名 余剰金、黒字 ★★★
[sə́:rpləs]

merchandise 名 品物、商品 ★★★
[mə́:rtʃəndàiz]

customs-cleared 形 税関を通過した ★★★
[kʌ́stəmzklìərd]

日本語訳

質問1～2は、次の記事に関するものです。

ソウル発--火曜日に、韓国中央銀行が、韓国の当座預金余剰額が、先月、1年前の20.3億ドルから11.7億ドルに急落したことを発表した。

　当座預金は、商品やサービスの貿易の大まかな尺度となるものである。

　中央銀行によると、今年最初の10ヶ月間の当座預金余剰額は、昨年の同じ期間の208.3億ドルから、86.5億ドルに落ちた。

　貿易黒字は、輸入が増え輸出が伸び悩んだことから、先月、1年前の黒字額26.2億ドルから15.3億ドルに落ちた。

　税関を通過した輸入は、10月に24.1％増えたが、輸出は14.7％しか伸びなかった。

Q1 先月の貿易黒字はいくらでしたか。
　(A) 11.7億ドル
　(B) 15.3億ドル
　(C) 20.3億ドル
　(D) 26.2億ドル

Q2 この記事からどんなことがわかりますか。
　(A) 今年の輸出は去年より伸びている。
　(B) 当座預金は、もっとも重要な経済指標である。
　(C) 昨年の経済は、今年よりよかった。
　(D) 韓国の経済は、今年改善している。

解答・解説 — answer and explanation

Answer 1 (B)

第4パラグラフに、The trade surplus fell to a surplus of 1.53 billion dollars last month, とあるので、先月の貿易黒字は、(B) の15.3億ドルであることがわかる。

Answer 2 (C)

今年になり、当座預金余剰額が昨年より減り、貿易黒字も昨年より減ったことから、今年より昨年の方が経済がよかったことがわかるので、(C) を選ぶ。

覚えてトクする語彙

merchant 名 商人 ★★★
merchandising 名 商品化計画 ★★★
customs 名 税関《複数扱い》 ★★★
clear 動 (税関など) を (正式手続きを終え) 通過する ★★★

Questions 1-2 refer to the following graph.

What do people at work do on the Internet during work hours? In a recent United States Internet usage survey (see bar graph below), fifty six percent of people interviewed said they spent approximately one-hour accessing non-work-related sites during work hours each week. A further fifteen percent said they use the Internet for non-work related activities approximately two hours a week. In secret monitoring, the most favored non-work related activity for us Inland Revenue Service Employees was going to financial sites. A close second to financial sites was accessing chat sites and doing e-mails, followed by miscellaneous activities.

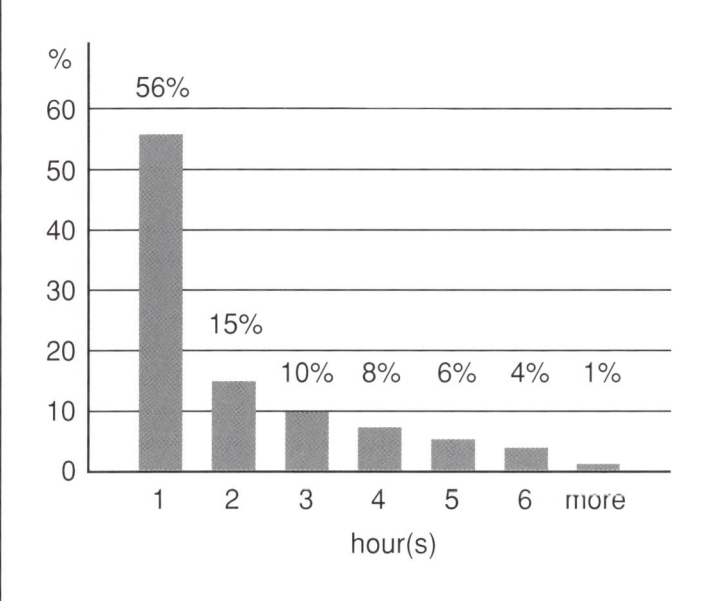

Accessing Non-work Related Internet Sites During Work Hours

Q1　What is the percentage of people who use the Internet for non-work related activities more than four hours a week?
　　(A) 18%
　　(B) 19%
　　(C) 28%
　　(D) 29%

Q2　What is the most favored non-work-related Internet activity that Inland Revenue Employees like to do while at work?
　　(A) Checking chat sites
　　(B) Doing e-mails
　　(C) Checking their personal finances
　　(D) Doing miscellaneous activities

《語彙のヒント》

usage 名 使い方、取り扱い方、慣習　★★★
[júːsidʒ]
bar graph 名 棒グラフ（= bar chart）　★★★
[báːr grǽf]
monitoring 名 監視、観察　★★★
[mánətəriŋ]
miscellaneous 形 種々雑多なものからなる、多方面の　★★★
[mìsəléiniəs]

日本語訳

質問1～2は次のグラフに関するものです。

勤務時間中、職場で人々はインターネットで何をしているのでしょう？　最近のアメリカインターネット使用調査（下の棒グラフ参照）によると、インタビューを受けた56％の人が毎週勤務時間中に仕事とは関係のないサイトに約1時間アクセスしているそうです。さらに15％の人が、1週間に約2時間、仕事に関係のないインターネットサイトを使っています。内密の監視によると、我がインランド・レベニュー・サービスの従業員の最も好む仕事と関係のないサイトは、金融サイトです。少差で金融サイトに次ぐのは、チャットサイトと電子メールで、次にその他が続きます。

（グラフ入る）

仕事と無関係なインターネットサイトへの勤務時間内アクセス

Q1　1週間に4時間以上、仕事と関係のないインターネット活動をしている人は何パーセントですか。
(A) 18％
(B) 19％
(C) 28％
(D) 29％

Q2　インランド・レベニュー・サービスの従業員が勤務時間中、もっとも好む仕事と関係のないインターネット活動はどれですか。
(A) チャットサイトをチェックする
(B) 電子メールをする
(C) 個人の金融をチェックする
(D) そのほか雑多な活動をする

第3章 ● パート7 読解問題（1つの文書）

解答・解説　　　　　　　　　　　　　　　　　　　　　　　answer and explanation

Answer 1　　　　　　　　　　　　　　　　　　　　　　　　　　　　　　　　（B）

グラフから、4時間以上仕事と関係のないインターネット活動をしている人は、8％＋6％＋4％＋1％＝19％なので、（B）が正解である。

Answer 2　　　　　　　　　　　　　　　　　　　　　　　　　　　　　　　　（C）

パッセージの最後の方に、the most favored non-work related activity for us Inland Revenue Service Employees was going to financial sites. とあるので、もっとも好まれているのは、（C）の「個人の金融をチェックする」ということになる。

覚えてトクする語彙

line-graph 名 折れ線グラフ　★★★
pie chart 名 円グラフ（＝ circle graph）　★★★
monitor 動 …を監視する　名 監視装置　★★★
monitory 形 警告の　★★☆

Questions 1-2 refer to the following memorandum.

MEMORANDUM

To: All Departments
From: Richard Brookes, Director *RB*
Re: Talking to the media
Date: July 23

Following the announcement of unexpected losses over the last six months, our Public Relations Office has been overrun with questions from the media. All staff are reminded that any statements about this firm must go through our Public Relations Office. Communication with the media in any other way is unacceptable.

All staff will remember the kind of confusion caused last year, when the media received contradictory statements about our financial situation. We need but one voice, and that is the voice of our Pubic Relations Office.

Q1 Why was the memo written to staff?
   (A) To encourage staff to speak to the media
   (B) To reprimand people who spoke to the media
   (C) To make contact with the Pubic Relations Office
   (D) To tell staff how to communicate with the media

Q2 According to the memo, what happened last year?
   (A) The unexpected loss was caused by the Public Relations Office.
   (B) Announcements to the media were done only by Public Relations Office.
   (C) All staff members were confused with the financial situation.
   (D) The media were given different information about the firm.

《語彙のヒント》

be overrun with ～ 熟 …で覆われてる、…がはびこっている ★★★
[bi òuvərrʌ́n wəð]

media 名 マスメディア、マスコミ（= mass media） ★★★
[míːdiə]

staff 名 《集合的》職員、社員 ★★★
[stǽf]

statement 名 声明、発表 ★★★
[stéitmənt]

unacceptable 形 容認できない、許されない ★★★
[ʌ̀nækséptəbl]

contradictory 形 矛盾する ★★★
[kɑ̀ntrədíktəri]

Public Relations Office 名 広報課 ★★★
[pʌ́blik riléiʃənz ɔ́ːfis]

reprimand 動 …を叱責する、非難する 名 叱責、非難 ★★★
[réprəmænd]

■ 日本語訳

translation

質問1～2は次の社内回覧に関するものです。

社内回覧

宛先：すべての部署
送信人：リチャード・ブルックス部長
用件：マスコミとの対話
日付：7月23日

ここ6ヶ月間にわたる予期せぬ損失に関する発表について、広報課はマスコミから質問攻めにあっています。我が社に関するコメントは、必ず広報課を通すようスタッフ全員再確認をお願いします。その他の方法では、決してマスコミとコンタクトを取らないでください。

昨年、財政状況に関してマスコミが矛盾したコメントを受け取り、混乱を招いたことを思い出してください。窓口は必要ですが、広報課ひとつだけでよいのです。

Q1 この社内回覧の目的は何ですか。
　　(A) 職員がマスコミと話すのを奨励するため
　　(B) マスコミと話した職員を非難するため
　　(C) 広報課とコンタクトを取るため
　　(D) マスコミとのコミュニケーションの取り方を職員に告げるため

Q2 この社内回覧によると、去年起こったことは何ですか。
　　(A) 広報課によって、予想外の損失が生じた。
　　(B) マスコミへの知らせは、すべて広報課によって行われた。
　　(C) すべての職員が財政状況に混乱した。
　　(D) マスコミは会社について異なる情報を与えられた。

第3章 ● パート7 読解問題（1つの文書）

解答・解説　　　　　　　　　　　　　　　　　　　　　　answer and explanation

Answer 1　　　　　　　　　　　　　　　　　　　　　　　　　　　　　　　　　　（D）
第1段落に、社に関するコメントは、必ず広報部を通し、その他の方法では、決してマスコミとコンタクトを取らないようにと書いてあるので、マスコミとのコンタクトの取り方を職員に徹底させるために書かれたメモであることがわかる。よって、（D）が正解となる。

Answer 2　　　　　　　　　　　　　　　　　　　　　　　　　　　　　　　　　　（D）
第2段落に the kind of confusion caused last year, when the media received contradictory statements about our financial situation とあり、マスコミが矛盾する異なる情報を得たことがわかるので、正解は（D）である。

覚えてトクする語彙

overrun 動 …を荒廃させる、圧倒する　★★★
staff member 名 一職員　★★★
staff agency 名 人材派遣会社　★★★
staff training 名 社員研修　★★★
staff transfer 名 人事異動　★★★
state 動 …をはっきり述べる、公表する　★★★
stated 形 定まった、一定の、はっきり述べられた　★★★
acceptable 形 受け取るにふさわしい、歓迎すべき　★★★
accept 動 …を受け取る、容認する　★★★
acceptance 名 承認、是認　★★★
acceptability 名 受け入れられること、満足なこと　★★★
accepted 形 容認された、認められている　★★★
acceptant 形 進んで受け入れる、受け入れやすい　★★★
contradiction 名 矛盾　★★★
contradict 動 …をきっぱりと否定する、…と矛盾する　★★★
contravene 動 （法律・習慣など）を破る　★★★
contraband 名 輸出入禁止品　★★★
contraception 名 避妊（法）　★★★
public relations 名 広報　★★★

Questions 1-2 refer to the following magazine article.

Researchers say one to two 1-cup servings daily of yogurt with probiotics are enough to be beneficial for adults. Children should stick to one cup of yogurt each day. "I think a probiotic a day is like a multivitamin a day. It offers protection against viruses," says Rosemary Young, pediatric gastroenterology nurse specialist.

Probiotics are added to — or found in — such foods as some rice and soy "milks" as well as acidophilus milks, yogurt, and some cottage cheese. If the products contain probiotics, they will be listed on the label, typically as acidophilus or bifidus.

Yogurt, drinkable yogurt, or fermented milk that lists probiotics on the label are among the best food sources of the helpful bacteria.

Besides foods, probiotics are sold in pills, powders, and suppositories. But experts caution that dietary supplements are not closely regulated, so there is no guarantee that the labels are accurate.

Q1 What is the purpose of the article?
   (A) To encourage children to eat yogurt everyday
   (B) To introduce a way to protect a body from viruses
   (C) To explain the structure and functions of probiotics
   (D) To inform people of the importance of bacteria

Q2 Which of the following is NOT suggested by the writer?
   (A) Eat yogurt with probiotics as much as possible every day
   (B) Choose yogurts which list probiotics on the label
   (C) Consume foods which contain acidophilus or bifidus
   (D) Be careful about the information on the labels of dietary supplements

《語彙のヒント》

yogurt 名 ヨーグルト ★★★
[jóugərt]

probiotics 名 プロバイオティックス（腸に働いて人の体にいろいろなよい働きをする微生物） ★★★
[prəbaiátiks]

stick 動 くっつく、くっついて離れない《to, on》 ★★★
[stík]

multivitamin 名 総合ビタミン剤 ★★★
[mÀltiváitəmin]

virus 名 ウイルス、ビールス ★★★
[váiərəs]

pediatric 形 小児科の ★★★
[pìdiætrik]

gastroenterology 名 消化器病学、胃腸病学 ★★★
[gæ̀strouèntərálədʒi]

acidophilus milk 名 乳酸菌牛乳 ★★★
[æ̀sədáfələs mílk]

bifidus 名 ビフィダス菌 ★★★
[bífidəs]

ferment 動 …を発酵させる ★★★
[fərmént]

suppository 名 座薬 ★★★
[səpázətɔ̀:ri]

caution 動 …であると事前に注意する、警告する 名 注意、用心 ★★★
[kɔ́:ʃən]

supplement 名 補足 ★★★
[sÁpləmənt]

regulate 動 …を規制する、統制する ★★★
[régjulèit]

guarantee 名 保証 動 …を保証する ★★★
[gæ̀rəntí:]

日本語訳

質問1〜2は、次の記事に関するものです。

毎日1〜2回1カップのプロバイオティックス入りヨーグルトは、成人にとって十分有益であると、研究者は言っている。子供は、1カップのヨーグルトを1日おきに食べるとよい。「毎日プロバイオティックスを取ることは、毎日マルチビタミンを取るようなものだ。プロバイオティックスは、ウイルスから体を守ってくれる」と小児科消化器病学看護専門士のローズマリー・ヤング氏は言っている。

プロバイオティックスは、米乳・豆乳・乳酸菌牛乳・ヨーグルト・カッテージチーズなどに含まれている。製品にプロバイオティックスが含まれていれば、乳酸菌・ビフィダス菌などと表示されている。

プロバイオティックスの表示のあるヨーグルト・飲むタイプのヨーグルト・発酵牛乳などは、有益なバクテリアを摂取するのに最適の食品である。

プロバイオティックスは、食品のほかに、錠剤・粉末・座薬としても売られている。しかし、栄養補助食品は規制が甘く表示が正確だという保証はないので、注意するよう専門家は呼びかけている。

Q1 この記事の目的は何ですか。
(A) 子供にヨーグルトを毎日食べるよう奨励する
(B) ウイルスから体を守る方法を紹介する
(C) プロバイオティックスの構造や働きを説明する
(D) バクテリアの重要性を人々に知らせる

Q2 筆者が提案していないのは次のどれですか。
(A) プロバイオティックスを含むヨーグルトを毎日できるだけたくさん食べる
(B) ラベルにプロバイオティックスが表示されているヨーグルトを選ぶ
(C) 乳酸菌やビフィダス菌を含む食物を食べる
(D) 栄養補助食品のラベルの情報に注意する

第3章 ● パート7 読解問題（1つの文書）

解答・解説 *answer and explanation*

Answer 1 (B)

子供は1日おきに食べることを奨励しているので、(A) は不可である。プロバイオティックスの構造は説明されていないので、(C) も不可である。バクテリアの重要性もとりたてて説明されていないので、(D) も不可である。ウイルスから体を守ることができるため、プロバイオティックスの摂取を勧める内容なので、(B) が正解である。

Answer 2 (A)

プロバイオティックスを含むヨーグルトを毎日1カップ食べることは提案されているが、できるだけたくさん食べようとは言っていないので、(A) が正解である。

覚えてトクする語彙

pediatrics 名 小児科学 ★★★
pediatrician 名 小児科医 ★★★
gastrology 名 胃（病）学 ★★★
gastrointestinal 形 胃腸の ★★★
gastroenteritis 名 胃腸炎 ★★★
fermentable 形 発酵性の ★★★
fermentation 名 発酵 ★★★
cautious 形 注意深い、用心深い ★★★
cautiousness 名 用心深さ ★★★
cautionary 形 注意・警戒を促す ★★★
supplementary 形 補遺の、増補の、追加の ★★★
regulation 名 規制、統制 ★★★
regulative 形 取締りの、規定する ★★★
regulatory 形 取り締まる、規定する ★★★
regulator 名 取締り人、規制者 ★★★

Questions 1 to 2 refer to the following advertisement.

Imagine being about to find out about young, emerging public growth companies before the Wall Street crowd moves in. We live in a time when the power of information has an incredible influence on the stock market. THE STOCK JOURNAL will make you aware of these undiscovered companies before Marketing Direct Concepts undertakes a national marketing recognition program designed to expose their enormous potential to the world.

Take the opportunity to learn about these unrecognized, undervalued companies with unique products and services. The successful execution of their business goals in conjunction with our national marketing campaign should have a dramatic effect on the valuation of their stock.

Whether you are a novice or seasoned investor, you can benefit from THE STOCK JOURNAL.

Turn the page, and you will find a sample of some of the companies covered by THE STOCK JOURNAL.

And now, for a limited time only, you can get a current list of all the undervalued companies in this program simply by calling this toll free number to receive a free trial subscription to:

> THE STOCK JOURNAL
> 1-888-795-421
> Visit our Web Site today at:
> www.stockjournal.com

Q1　Who would be most interested in THE STOCK JOURNAL?
　　(A) Someone who wants to start a new business on Wall Street
　　(B) Someone who wants to invest money in undervalued companies
　　(C) Someone who wants to buy stocks of companies doing well
　　(D) Someone who wants to learn about unique products and services

Q2　What should you do to get a list of all the underestimated companies?
　　(A) Turn the page
　　(B) Call the toll free number
　　(C) Access to the web site
　　(D) Visit the company

《語彙のヒント》

undervalue 動 …を過小評価する、軽視する ★★★
[ʌ̀ndərvǽljuː]
execution 名 （義務・目的などの）実行、遂行 ★★★
[èksikjúːʃən]
conjunction 名 結合・連結すること、共同、関連、接続詞 ★★★
[kəndʒʌ́ŋkʃən]
valuation 名 （金銭的）評価すること、査定、見積り、評価額、査定額 ★★★
[væ̀ljuéiʃən]
novice 名 初心者（= beginner）★★★
[návis]
seasoned 形 よく慣れた、ベテランの ★★★
[síːznd]
subscription 名 購読 ★★★
[səbskrípʃən]

日本語訳

質問1～2は、次の記事に関するものです。

ウオール・ストリートの連中が入り込む前に、新しく出現し成長している会社をこれから見つけようとしているところを想像してみてください。我々は今、強力な情報が、株式市場に信じられない影響を及ぼす時代に生きています。THE STOCK JOURNAL は、大きな可能性を世界に知らせるために作られた国営マーケティング認定プログラムにマーケティング・ディレクト・コンセプトが着手する前に、未だ発見されていない会社をあなたに気づかせてくれます。

これら未認定の過小評価されているユニークな製品やサービスを提供する会社について学ぶ機会を得てください。これらの会社の目的が達成されれば、わが国のマーケティングキャンペーンと連動して、これらの会社の株の価値に劇的な影響を与えるでしょう。

あなたが初心者であれベテラン投資家であれ、THE STOCK JOURNAL から利益を得ることができます。

ページをめくってください。THE STOCK JOURNAL にカバーされた会社のいくつかの例が載っています。

そして今、限られた期間のみ、過小評価されている会社すべてのリストを手にすることができます。以下のフリーダイアルに電話して、無料お試し購読をお受け取りください。

> THE STOCK JOURNAL
> 1-888-795-421
> ホームページも今すぐご覧ください。
> www.stockjournal.com

Q1 THE STOCK JOURNAL に最も興味を抱く人は誰ですか。
(A) ウオールストリートで新しいビジネスを始めたい人
(B) 過小評価されている会社にお金を投資したい人
(C) 業績のよい会社の株を買いたい人
(D) ユニークな製品やサービスについて学びたい人

Q2 過小評価されているすべての会社のリストを手に入れたければ、どうしたらよいですか。
(A) ページをめくる
(B) フリーダイアルに電話する
(C) ホームページにアクセスする
(D) 会社を訪ねる

解答・解説

Answer 1 (B)

THE STOCK JOURNAL は、まだ評価されていないユニークな製品やサービスを提供している会社を紹介する雑誌なので、(B) が正解である。

Answer 2 (B)

最後の段落に、you can get a current list of all the undervalued companies in this program simply by calling this toll free number to receive a free trial subscription to: とあるので、正解は (B) である。

覚えてトクする語彙

- **emergence** 名 出現 ★★★
- **emergency** 名 緊急事態 ★★★
- **emergent** 形 現れ出る、緊急の ★★★
- **understate** 動 …を控えめに述べる ★★★
- **undermine** 動 …を弱体化する、傷つける ★★★
- **underestimate** 動 …を過小評価する ★★★
- **undercut** 動 (競争者よりも) 安く売る ★★★
- **execute** 動 …を実行する、実施する ★★★
- **conjunct** 形 (…と) 結合・連結した、共同の 《with》 ★★★
- **conjunctive** 形 連結・結合する、共同の ★★★
- **valuate** 動 …を評価する、見積もる ★★★
- **valuator** 名 評価する人 ★★★
- **subscribe** 動 購読する ★★★

Questions 1-2 refer to the following recipe.

LEMON-BLACKBERRY MINITARTS

1/2 of a 15-oz. pkg. folded refrigerated unbaked piecrust (1 crust)
1/2 of an 8-oz. pkg. cream cheese, softened
1/4 cup purchased lemon curd
1 cup fresh blackberries
2 tbsp. seedless blackberry
spreadable fruit
2 tbsp. lemon juice
4 mint sprigs
Powdered sugar

1. Let piecrust stand at room temperature 15 minutes. Preheat oven to 400 °F. Unfold piecrust. Cut four 4 1/2- to 5-inch rounds from piecrust. Press rounds firmly into bottom and up sides of four 3 1/2- to 4-inch individual tart pans with removable bottoms. Trim crusts even with top of pans. Prick bottoms of each crust several times with tines of a fork. Place pans on a baking sheet. Bake for 10 to 20 minutes or until golden brown. Cool completely on a wire rack.
2. In a small mixing bowl beat cream cheese and lemon curd with an electric mixer on medium speed until smooth. Divide filling among pastry shells, spreading evenly. Cover; refrigerate 2 hours until chilled. Before serving, remove from pans; place tarts on plates. Arrange berries on each tart. Combine spreadable fruit and lemon juice; spoon over tarts. Add a mint sprig, and sift powdered sugar over tops. Serves 4.

Q1 What do you have to do before the tart pans are put in the oven?
(A) Beat each crust several times
(B) Cut the top of the crusts
(C) Place the tart pans in fridge
(D) Put filling in tart pans

Q2 Which of the following is NOT put on the tart?
(A) Berries
(B) Lemon peel
(C) Mint sprig
(D) Sugar

《語彙のヒント》

blackberry 名 黒イチゴ ★★★
[blǽkbèri]

oz. 名 オンス、1oz. = 28.3495g (= ounce) ★★★
[áuns]

pkg. 名 包み (= package) ★★★
[pǽkidʒ]

folded refrigerated unbaked piecrust 名 冷凍パイ生地
(平べったいパイ生地が幾重にか折られていて、それを広げて使用する) ★★★
[fóuldid rifrídʒərèitid ʌnbéikt páikrʌ̀st]

curd 名 凝乳、凝乳状の食品 ★★★
[kə́ːrd]

tbsp. 名 テーブルスプーン (= tablespoon, table spoonful 〈tbs と省略することもある〉) ★★★
[téiblspùːn]

seedless 形 種なしの ★★★
[síːdles]

spreadable 形 (塗り) 広げられる ★★★
[sprédəbl]

sprig 名 小枝、若枝 ★★★
[spríg]

powdered sugar 名 粉末状グラニュー糖 ★★★
[páudərd ʃúgər]

pan 名 オーブン用の皿 ★★★
[pæn]

trim 動 …(余分なものなど)を切り取る ★★★
[trím]

prick 動 …をちくりと刺す、…に小穴をあける ★★★
[prík]

tine 名 (フォークなどの)とがった先 ★★★
[táin]

beat 動 …を強くかきまぜる、泡立てる、打つ、たたく ★★★
[bíːt]

filling 名 詰め物、具 ★★★
[fíliŋ]

pastry 名 ペーストリー(パイ・タルトなどのケーキ・菓子) ★★★
[péistri]

shell 名 (ケーキの)皮、(果物・ピーナツなどの)殻 ★★★
[ʃél]

lemon peel 名 (砂糖漬けの)レモンの皮 ★★★
[lémən pìːl]

日本語訳

質問1〜2は、次のレシピに関するものです。

レモンと黒イチゴのミニタルト

15オンスの冷凍パン生地 1/2
8オンスのクリームチーズ 1/2、やわらかくしておく
市販のレモン凝固剤 1/4カップ
新鮮な黒イチゴ 1カップ
種無し黒いちごスプーン 2
細かくしたフルーツ
レモン汁スプーン 2
ミント 4本
粉末状グラニュー糖

1. パイ生地を室内温度で15分おく。オーブンを華氏400度で予熱する。パイ生地を広げる。パイ生地を4つにそれぞれ4 1/2から5インチになるよう切る。生地を1つずつ3 1/2から4インチのタルト皿に入れ、底と横にしっかりと押し当てる。皿からはみ出た生地は上がそろうように切り取る。フォークの先のとがった部分

で、底の生地を数回刺す。ベーキング・シートの上に皿を置く。金茶色になるまで、10〜20分焼く。ワイヤー・ラックの上に置き、完全に冷ます。
2. 小さなボールに、クリーム・チーズとレモン凝固剤を入れ、やわらかくなるまで中スピードの泡だて器でかきまぜる。混ぜ終わったものを4等分し、1でできたタルト皮に入れる。覆いをし、冷蔵庫で2時間冷却する。タルト皿からタルトを取り、タルトを皿の上に置く。タルトの上にイチゴをのせる。細かくしたフルーツとレモン汁を合わせる。タルトの上にスプーンですくってのせる。ミントの葉をのせ、上に粉砂糖をふりかける。4人前。

Q1 タルト皿をオーブンに入れる前にしなければならないことは何ですか。
　(A) それぞれのパイ生地を何回かこねる
　(B) パイ生地の上を切る
　(C) タルト皿を冷蔵庫に入れる
　(D) タルト皿に詰め物を入れる

Q2 タルトの上に置かれないものは次のどれですか。
　(A) ベリー
　(B) レモンの皮
　(C) ミントの葉
　(D) 砂糖

解答・解説

Answer 1 (B)
1の最後の方に Bake for 10 to 20 minutes 〜とあり、それ以前のところを見ると、Trim crusts even with top of pans. とあるので、(B) が正解となる。

Answer 2 (B)
2の最後の方に、Arrange berries、Add a mint spring、shift powdered sugar とあり、(B) のレモンの皮だけは書かれていないので、(B) が正解となる。

覚えてトクする語彙

berry [名] ベリー（イチゴの類など核のない食用小果実）　★★★
fold [動] …を折る　★★★
unfold [動]（折りたたんだもの）を広げる、開ける　★★★
piecrust [名] パイ生地、パイ皮　★★★
bean curd [名] 豆腐　★★★
seed [名] 種　★★★
spread [動] …を広げる　★★★
peel [名]（果物などの）皮　[動] …の皮をむく　★★★

Questions 1 to 5 refer to the following two e-mails.

To: Customer Relations Department
From: Alexander McDonald
Subject: PO#51802

The items covered by our purchase order, PO#51802, placed on March 10 were supposed to have been delivered by the end of the month but, as of April 4, we have not received them. We need to supply them to our customers by April 15. If the shipment does not arrive immediately, we may lose their custom. Please advise the current status of this order as soon as possible.

Regards,

A. McDonald

To: Alexander McDonald
From: Edward Hill, Manager, Customer Relations Department
Subject: Re: PO#51802

Dear Mr. McDonald:

Thank you for your e-mail of April 4 bringing the problem of late delivery to our attention. We fully understand your frustration.

As much as we would like to help you, the problem lies with the trucking firm. We have contacted them concerning the late delivery and are reviewing our use of Carlton Trucking as our carrier. We are insisting that they expedite delivery of this order immediately. Would it be possible for you to contact them, also, to emphasize the seriousness of the situation? The telephone number is 311-458-1448, and the relevant invoice is CT001067.

We can assure you that we are trying our hardest to remedy the situation as quickly as we can. Unfortunately, an immediate solution is dependent upon Carlton Trucking. Thank you for your patience and understanding. We hope this problem is resolved soonest.

Regards,

Edward Hill
Manager, Customer Relations Department

Q1 When did Alexander McDonald send the e-mail to Edward Hill?
 (A) March 10
 (B) March 31
 (C) April 4
 (D) April 15

Q2 What is the purpose of Alexander McDonald's e-mail?
 (A) To order items
 (B) To cancel the order
 (C) To make a claim
 (D) To ask about an order

Q3 What does Edward Hill probably want Carlton Trucking to do?
 (A) He wants them to make a contract immediately.
 (B) He wants them to end the contract.
 (C) He wants them to effect delivery.
 (D) He wants them to emphasize McDonald's situation.

Q4 What will Edward Hill probably do about Alexander McDonald's order?
 (A) He will send the items immediately.
 (B) He will solve McDonald's problem.
 (C) He will ask Carlton Trucking to help McDonald.
 (D) He will do nothing.

Q5 Who can solve McDonald's problem?
 (A) Carlton Trucking
 (B) Edward Hill
 (C) McDonald himself
 (D) Customer Relations Department

《語彙のヒント》

as of 形 …現在では ★★★
[əz əv]

shipment 名 発送品、出荷、発送 ★★★
[ʃípmənt]

custom 名 取引（先） ★★★
[kʌ́stəm]

trucking firm 名 運送会社 ★★☆
[trʌ́kiŋ fə̀ːrm]

carrier 名 運送業者、配達人 ★★☆
[kǽriər]

insist 動 …を要求する、主張する ★★★
[insíst]

expedite 動 …を急送する、はかどらせる ★★★
[ékspədàit]

invoice 名 送り状、納品伝票 ★★★
[ínvɔis]

remedy 動 …を改善する ★★★
[rémədi]

effect 動 …を達成する ★★☆
[ifékt]

日本語訳

問題1～5は次の2つのメールに関するものです。

宛先：顧客サービス部門
差出人：アレキサンダー・マクドナルド
件名：注文番号51802

3月10日に注文しました注文番号51802の商品が3月中に届くはずでしたが、4月4日現在、まだ受け取っておりません。4月15日までに顧客に納品しなければなりません。すぐに商品が届かなければ、取引先を失いかねません。早急に出荷の状況をお知らせください。

よろしくお願いいたします。

A. マクドナルド

宛先：アレキサンダー・マクドナルド
差出人：エドワード・ヒル、顧客サービス部門部長
用件：Re：注文番号51802

4月4日付けのメールで遅配の問題をご指摘いただきありがとうございます。貴社の苛立ちはよくわかります。

できる限りのお手伝いをしたいところではありますが、問題は運送会社にございます。遅配については運送会社に連絡し、カールトン運送に委託している弊社の配送状況について見直しを行っております。私共は、カールトン運送にご注文の品を急送するよう強く要求し続けております。できましたら貴社側からも、カールトン運送に事態の深刻さを強調していただけないでしょうか。電話番号は311-458-1448、送り状はCT001067です。

弊社がこの状況をできるだけ敏速に解決すべく懸命に取り組んでいることは間違いございません。しかし、残念ながら、今回の解決はカールトン運送に委ねられております。ご忍耐、ご理解に感謝いたします。この問題が、ただちに解決されますよう願ってやみません。

敬具

エドワード・ヒル
顧客サービス部門、部長

第3章 ● パート7 読解問題（2つの文書）

Q1 アレキサンダー・マクドナルドは、いつエドワード・ヒルに電子メールを送りましたか。
(A) 3月10日
(B) 3月31日
(C) 4月4日
(D) 4月15日

Q2 アレキサンダー・マクドナルドが電子メールを送った目的は何ですか。
(A) 品物を注文するため
(B) 注文を取り消すため
(C) クレームをつけるため
(D) 注文について尋ねるため

Q3 エドワード・ヒルはカールトン運送にどうしてほしいのですか。
(A) すぐに契約を締結してほしい。
(B) 契約を打ち切ってほしい。
(C) 配送をしてほしい。
(D) マクドナルド氏の状況を強調してほしい。

Q4 アレキサンダー・マクドナルドの注文に関して、エドワード・ヒルはどうするでしょうか。
(A) 品物をすぐに送る。
(B) マクドナルド氏の問題を解決する。
(C) カールトン運送にマクドナルド氏を助けるよう求める。
(D) 何もしない。

Q5 だれがマクドナルド氏の問題を解決できますか。
(A) カールトン運送
(B) エドワード・ヒル
(C) マクドナルド本人
(D) 顧客サービス部門

解答・解説   answer and explanation

Answer 1   (C)
マクドナルド氏のメールでも「4月4日現在」とあり、ヒル氏のメールにも「4月4日付けのメール」となっているので、正解は (C) である。

Answer 2   (D)
マクドナルド氏は注文した品を期限までに受け取っておらず、マクドナルド氏のメールの最後に Please advise the current status of this order as soon as possible. とあるので、注文がどうなっているのか問い合わせているのである。よって、正解は (D) となる。

Answer 3   (C)
ヒル氏はカールトン運送にこの遅配の件に関して問い合わせ、かつすぐに配送するように強く言い続けているのだから、正解は (C) である。

Answer 4   (C)
ヒル氏のメールに We are insisting that they expedite delivery of this order immediately. とあり、現在進行形を使っているので、今後もカールトン運送に早急に配送するよう訴え続けると考えられる。よって、正解は (C) となる。

Answer 5   (A)
ヒル氏のメールに the problem lies with the trucking firm、an immediate solution is dependent upon Carlton Trucking とあるので、問題を解決できるのはカールトン運送のみである。よって、正解は (A) となる。

覚えてトクする語彙

shipping 名 出荷、発送、輸送 ★★★
insistence 名 強い主張、断言 ★★★
insistent 形 主張する《on, upon, about》、要求などがしつこい ★★★
expedition 名 迅速さ ★★★
remedial 形 治療のための、矯正の、補習の ★★★
remediable 形 治せる、治療できる ★★★
effective 形 効果的な ★★★

Questions 1 to 5 refer to the following e-mail message and program.

To: Mr. Tom Shaw, Director of Chemical Department, Thomas Disposal Company
From: Milton Allan, Program Manager
Subject: Re: Conference Schedule
Date: April 5, 2006

Dear Mr. Shaw,

Thank you very much for your inquiry concerning our conference. I hope the attached information will be of use to you. If you need more detailed information, a brochure will be available at $15. Please let me know by return email if you would like one mailed to you. We strongly recommend that you register for the conference soon. If you register one month in advance, the admission fee will be reduced by 10 %. Also, there are not many hotels near the conference hall and already some of them are fully booked for the relevant dates. To register for the conference, drop me an email. For further information, please call 231-835-3496 during business hours Monday through Friday from 9:00 a.m. to 6:00 p.m. We are looking forward to seeing you at the conference.

Best regards,
Milton Allan

14th International Industrial Waste Conference
May 13- 14, 2006
Admission: $80 for 2 Day Pass, $50 per day

Saturday, May 13, 2006

1:00 p.m. - 2:00 p.m.　Registration

2:00 p.m. - 2:20 p.m.　Welcome and Opening Remarks
   Dr. Brian Larsen, Chancellor, Freeman University
   Dr. Paul Maurer, President, Northwest Evergreen Corp.

2:20 p.m. - 3:00 p.m.　Keynote Address
   Dr. John Phillips, Dean, University of Southeastern California, Department of Ecology

3:00 p.m. - 3:20 p.m.　Afternoon Break

3:20 p.m. - 4:00 p.m.　Session 1: "Recycling Systems in the Petroleum Industry" Alicia Mclennan (Room1)
   "Reuse in the Steel Industry" Douglas Willis (Room 2)

4:10 p.m. - 4:50 p.m.　Session 2: "Arsenic and Carbon Chloride Regulation" Ted McNeill (Room 1)
   "New Offensive Odor Control" James Anderson (Room 2)

5:00 p.m. - 5:40 p.m.　Session 3: "Problems of Sewage Treatment" Marta Garcia (Room 1)
   "Dealing with Oil Spills" Daniel Young (Room 2)

6:00 p.m. - Reception　Sponsored by ICT Waste Industry Corp.

Sunday, May 14, 2006

9:00 a.m. - 9:30 a.m.　Registration

9:30 a.m. - 10:10 a.m.　Session 4: "Environmental Cooperation in Asia" Li You Wen & Masashi Tanaka (Room 1)
"Waste Treatment in Europe" Ivan Ivanov (Room 2)

10:20 a.m. - 11:00 a.m.　Session 5: "Issues in Regional Waste Disposal Landfill" Christian Hill (Room 1)
"An Example of an Eco-city" Ralph Kitamura (Room 2)

11:10 a.m. - 11:50 a.m.　Session 6: "Waste Incineration and Dioxin Issues" Erik Wright (Room 1)
"A Report on the Comprehensive Environmental Survey of Chemical Substances" Anita Moore (Room 2)

11:50 a.m. - 1:30 p.m.　Lunch Break

1:30 p.m. - 3:30 p.m.　Panel Discussion "Designing Zero Emission Systems"
　　Dr. Steve Bergman, Ronald University
　　Dr. Nancy Marion, Kellogg Environmental Center
　　Dr. Linda Barrow, University of Marine Affairs
　　Dr. Frank Widdowson, Environmental Ministry

3:30 p.m. - 4:00 p.m.　Closing Address
　　Dr. Angela Hong, Chairperson

Q1　Why did Mr. Milton send this email to Mr. Show?

(A) Mr. Milton wanted to advertise the conference.

(B) Mr. Show requested some information about the conference.

(C) Mr. Milton forgot to send Mr. Show the conference schedule before.

(D) Mr. Show needed to reserve a place to stay during the conference.

Q2　Who will most likely attend this conference?
　　(A) Scientists of an optical fiber company
　　(B) Representatives of a garment company
　　(C) Commissioners of a textile company
　　(D) Entrepreneurs of a pharmaceutical company

Q3　Who would most likely be interested in session five?
　　(A) Professors of international relations
　　(B) Chemists of a petrochemical company
　　(C) Engineers of an industrial waste management contractor
　　(D) Local government workers of environmental department

Q4　If Mr. Show registers for the conference for two days now, how much will the admission fee be?
　　(A) $72
　　(B) $80
　　(C) $90
　　(D) $100

Q5　What does Mr. Show have to do for early registration?
　　(A) He has to mail a letter.
　　(B) He has to write an email.
　　(C) He has to send the registration fee.
　　(D) He has to make a phone call.

《語彙のヒント》

disposal 名 処理 ★★★
[dispóuzəl]

attach 動 …を添付する、貼り付ける ★★★
[ətǽtʃ]

brochure 名 パンフレット、小冊子 ★★★
[brouʃúər]

register 動 登録する《for》 ★★★
[rédʒistər]

admission 名 入場料 ★★★
[ædmíʃən]

reduce 動 …を減らす ★★★
[ridjúːs]

relevant 形 関連がある ★★★
[réləvənt]

conference 名 会議、協議 ★★★
[kánfərəns]

remark 名 言葉、所見、見解 動 …と述べる ★★★
[rimáːrk]

ecology 名 生態（学） ★★★
[ikálədʒi]

petroleum 名 石油 ★★★
[pətróuliəm]

steel 名 鉄鋼 ★★★
[stíːl]

arsenic 名 ヒ素 ★★★
[áːrsənik]

carbon chloride 名 有機塩素化合物 ★★★
[káːrbən klɔ́ːraid]

offensive 形 不快な、無礼な、攻撃の ★★★
[əfénsiv]

odor 名 におい、臭気 ★★★
[óudər]

sewage 名 下水、汚水 ★★★
[súːidʒ]

spill 名 流出 動 …をこぼす ★★★
[spíl]

landfill 名 ごみ処理場 ★★★
[lǽndfìl]

incineration 名 焼却 ★★★
[insìnəréiʃən]

dioxin 名 ダイオキシン ★★★
[daiάksən]

emission 名 放出 ★★★
[imíʃən]

optical fiber 名 光ファイバー ★★★
[άptikəl fáibər]

garment 名 衣服 ★★★
[gάːrmənt]

commissioner 名 理事、委員 ★★★
[kəmíʃənər]

entrepreneur 名 企業家、請負人 ★★★
[ὰːntrəprənə́ːr]

pharmaceutical 形 薬剤の ★★★
[fὰːrməsúːtikəl]

petrochemical 形 石油化学の ★★★
[pètroukémikəl]

contractor 名 請負業者、(工事)請負人 ★★★
[kάntræktər]

日本語訳

質問1〜5は次の電子メールとプログラムに関するものです。

宛先：トム・ショウ・トーマス処理会社化学部部長
送信者：ミルトン・アラン・プログラム総括者
件名：Re：会議の予定表
日時：2006年4月5日

ショウ様

私どもの会議に関してのお問い合わせをありがとうございました。添付しました情報がお役に立つことを願っております。もっと詳細な情報がお入用でしたら、15ドルで小冊子を販売しております。お入用でしたら、メールでお知らせください。会議に参加される場合は、早急に登録されることをお勧めいたします。1ヶ月

前に登録されますと、参加費が10パーセント割引となります。また、会議場の近くにはあまりホテルがなく、いくつかのホテルはすでに満室となっております。会議参加の登録は、電子メールでお伝えください。ご質問がございましたら、月曜から金曜の午前9時から午後6時の営業時間内に、231-835-3496 までお電話ください。会議でお目にかかれることを楽しみにしております。

敬具
ミルトン・アラン

第14回国際産業廃棄会議
2006年5月13〜14日
参加費：80ドル（両日）、50ドル（1日）

2006年5月13日（土）
午後1時〜2時　受付
午後2時〜2時20分　開会式
　　　フリーマン大学総長ブライアン・ラーセン博士
　　　ノースウエストエバーグリーン会社ポール・マーレア社長
午後2時〜3時　基調講演
　　　サウスイースタンカリフォルニア大学生態学部学部長ジョン・フィリップス博士
午後3時〜3時20分　休憩
午後3時20分〜4時　第1セッション：「石油業界におけるリサイクルシステム」アリーシア・マクレナン（第1室）
　　　「鉄鋼業界における再利用」ダグラス・ウイリス（第2室）
午後4時10分〜4時50分　第2セッション：「ヒ素と有機化合物の規制」テッド・マクニル（第1室）
　　　「新悪臭防止法」ジェイムス・アンダーソン（第2室）
午後5時〜5時40分　第3セッション：「下水処理問題」マルタ・ガルシア（第1室）
　　　「石油流出の扱い」ダニエル・ヤング（第2室）
午後6時〜　懇親会　　ICT廃棄産業社後援

2006年5月14日（日）
午前9時〜9時30分　受付
午前9時30分〜10時10分　第4セッション：「アジアにおける環境協力」李友

　　　　　　文、田中正司（第1室）
　　　　　「ヨーロッパにおける廃棄物処理」イヴァン・イヴァノフ（第2室）
午前10時20分〜11時00分　第5セッション：「広域処分場問題」クリスチャ
　　　　ン・ヒル（第1室）
　　　　　「エコ・シティーの一例」ラルフ・キタムラ（第2室）
午前11時10分〜11時50分　第6セッション：「ごみ焼却とダイオキシン問題」
　　　　エリック・ライト（第1室）
　　　　　「化学物質環境安全性総点検調査報告」アニタ・ムーア（第2室）
午前11時50分〜1時30分　昼食休憩
午後1時30分〜3時30分　公開討論会「ゼロ・エミッションシステムの構想」
　　　　ロナルド大学 スティーブン・バーグマン博士
　　　　ケロッグ環境センター ナンシー・マリオン博士
　　　　マリン・アフェアーズ大学 リンダ・バロー博士
　　　　環境省 フランク・ウイドーソン博士
午後3時30分〜4時　閉会式
　　　　アンジェラ・ホン議長

Q1　ミルトン氏はなぜショウ氏にこのメールを送ったのですか。
　　(A)ミルトン氏が会議の宣伝をしたかったから。
　　(B)ショウ氏が会議の情報を求めたから。
　　(C)ミルトン氏がショウ氏に会議の予定表を送り忘れたから。
　　(D)ショウ氏は会議の間、滞在する場所を予約する必要があったから。

Q2　だれがこの会議に出席する可能性が最も高いですか。
　　(A)光ファイバー会社の科学者
　　(B)衣服会社の代表者
　　(C)繊維会社の理事
　　(D)製薬会社の企業家

Q3　だれが最も第5セッションに興味を抱くでしょうか。
　　(A)国際関係の教授
　　(B)石油化学会社に勤める化学者
　　(C)産業廃棄物業者の技師
　　(D)環境課の公務員

Q4 ショウ氏が今2日間の会議に登録すると、参加費はいくらになりますか。
(A) 72ドル
(B) 80ドル
(C) 90ドル
(D) 100ドル

Q5 ショウ氏が事前登録をするにはどうすればよいですか。
(A) 手紙を送る。
(B) 電子メールを送る。
(C) 参加費を納める。
(D) 電話をする。

解答・解説　　　　　　　　　　　　　　　　　　　　answer and explanation

Answer 1 (B)
電子メールの最初に Thank you very much for your inquiry of our conference. とあるので、ショウ氏がたずねた質問への返事だということがわかり、正解は (B) となる。

Answer 2 (D)
産業廃棄物の会議であるので、光ファイバー・衣類・繊維会社関係の人たちは、あまり関心がなく、もっとも可能性が高いのは製薬会社関連の人であると考えられるので、正解は (D) となる。

Answer 3 (D)
第5セッションの発表は、「広域処分場問題」と「エコ・シティーの一例」なので、公務員が一番興味を抱くと考えられる。よって、正解は (D) である。

Answer 4 (A)
1ヶ月前に登録をすれば10%割引されるので、80ドル－8ドル＝72ドルで、(A) が正解である。

Answer 5 (B)
電子メールに To register for the conference, drop me an email. とあるので、正解は (B) である。

覚えてトクする語彙

dispose 動 処分する《of》★★★
disposable 形 使い捨ての ★★★
attachment 名 添付ファイル、付属品 ★★★
admit 動 …を認める、許可する ★★★
admittance 名 入場許可 ★★★
reduction 名 減少 ★★★

reductive 形 減少する ★★★
relevance 名 (問題との) 関連 (性) ★★★
remarkable 名 注目すべき ★★★
remarkably 副 著しく ★★★
ecological 形 生態 (上) の、環境の、環境にやさしい ★★★
carbon dioxide 名 二酸化炭素 ★★★
incinerate 動 …を焼却する、焼いて灰にする ★★★
incinerator 名 (ごみなどの) 焼却炉 ★★★
emit 動 (熱・におい・光など) を放出する ★★★
commission 名 委任・委託、手数料 ★★★
pharmacy 名 調剤薬局 ★★★
pharmacist 名 薬剤師 ★★★

Questions 1 to 5 refer to the following advertisement and e-mail.

Smart Business Academy

Diploma in **Business & the Law** — A *new* six-month intensive course. This innovative diploma-level course has been carefully created from the foundation components of our world acclaimed **Master's of Business Administration** course. Successful completion of the Diploma in **Business & the Law** will entitle candidates for the **M.B.A** course to apply for credits equivalent to successfully completing the first year of full-time instruction on the master's course.

Choose 1 module from each group in addition to the core curriculum subjects of Accountancy, Management Theory, Marketing and Statistics.

Group 1
Corporate Citizenship
Information Technology
Mass Media
Public Relations

Group 2
International Law
Maritime Law
Environmental Law
Contract Law

For further information visit our website http://smarbusac.com
Email info@smarbusac.com or write for a prospectus and application form to Smart Business Academy, Edge Hill, Everpool, U.K. EPL 978

To	info@smarbusac.com
From	K. Izumi <ki@yamail.co.jp>
Subject	Diploma in Business & the Law

Dear Smart Business Academy,

I read your advertisement in The Weekly International and I am very interested in enrolling for the above course but I would appreciate some more information.

Is it possible to take both International Law and Maritime Law or may only one of these be chosen? I am employed by a large international shipping corporation, who have kindly agreed to meet the costs of tuition and to grant me the time for a six-month course of study, should I decide to engage in such a course. You may appreciate, that the two modules in different aspects of business and the law are extremely relevant to my employer and to myself. I would therefore, like to study both, if possible. Also, as I hold a Higher National Certificate in Accountancy, which I believe is of a higher level than the accountancy module in your Diploma in Business & the Law course, may I be exempted from the Accountancy module in favor of studying an extra module from Group 1? I intend to choose the Information Technology module but would be extremely pleased to additionally take the module in Corporate Citizenship.

Thank you in advance for all your help.

Regards,
Kunio Izumi

Q1　What happens when students have completed this six-month intensive course?
　　(A) They can receive an M.B.A.
　　(B) They must become a business administrator.
　　(C) They can apply for the M.B.A. program.
　　(D) They will be awarded an M.B.A.

Q2　Which student can complete the intensive course?
　　(A) A student who completed Accountancy, Management Theory, Marketing, Statistics, Mass Media, Public Relations
　　(B) A student who completed Management Theory, Marketing, Statistics, Mass Media, International Law
　　(C) A student who completed Accountancy, Management Theory, Statistics, Corporate Citizenship, Contract Law
　　(D) A student who completed Accountancy, Management Theory, Marketing, Statistics, Mass Media, Maritime Law

Q3　What does Mr. Izumi most likely do?
　　(A) He is a business major student.
　　(B) He is an employer of a company.
　　(C) He is an office worker.
　　(D) He is a lawyer of an academic institution.

Q4　How many questions did Mr. Izumi ask in his mail?
　　(A) One
　　(B) Two
　　(C) Three
　　(D) Four

Q5 Why does Mr. Izumi want to know if he may be exempted from the Accountancy module?
   (A) He wants to take more courses in Group 1.
   (B) He already has a qualification in accountancy.
   (C) He wants to take a higher level accountancy course.
   (D) He is planning to choose the Information Technology module.

《語彙のヒント》

diploma 名 修了（卒業）証書、(学科・大学院の) 学位 ★★★
[diplóumə]

intensive 形 集中的な ★★★
[inténsiv]

innovative 形 革新的な ★★★
[ínəvèitiv]

component 名 構成要素 ★★★
[kəmpóunənt]

acclaim 動 …を賞賛する 名 賞賛 ★★★
[əkléim]

entitle 動 …する資格（権利）を与える ★★★
[intáitl]

equivalent 形 同等の《to》 ★★★
[ikwívələnt]

module 名 大学の履修の単位（主に英）、モジュール、構成単位 ★★★
[mádʒuːl]

accountancy 名 経理、会計事務 ★★★
[əkáuntənsi]

public relations 名 広報 ★★★
[pʌ́blik reléiʃənz]

maritime 形 海事の、海の ★★★
[mǽrətàim]

prospectus 名 (学校・ホテルなどの) 案内書、(計画・事業などの) 趣意書 ★★★
[prəspéktəs]

enroll 動 …に入学・入会する ★★★
[inróul]

tuition 名 授業料 ★★★
[tjuːíʃən]

grant 動 (許可など) を与える 名 認可、授与 ★★★
[grǽnt]

certificate 名 証明書、免許状 ★★★
[sərtífikət]

exempt 動 …を免除する 形 免除された《from》 ★★★
[igzémpt]

administrator 名 管理者、行政官 ★★★
[ædmínəstrèitər]

award 動 (賞) を与える 名 賞、賞品 ★★★
[əwɔ́ːrd]

qualification 名 資格 ★★★
[kwàləfikéiʃən]

■ 日本語訳　　　　　　　　　　　　　　　　　　　　　　　　　　translation

質問 1 ～ 5 は次の広告と電子メールに関するものです。

<u>スマート・ビジネス・アカデミー</u>

ビジネス＆法律の資格免許 —— 6ヶ月の新集中講座

この革新的な学位レベルのコースは、世界でも評判の高い我々の経営学修士コースの基本的な要素から、入念に創られました。ビジネス＆法律の資格免許を取られた方は、経営学修士プログラムの応募資格が与えられ、経営修士学コース一年目の課程修了と同等の単位が取得できます。

<u>経理</u>、<u>経営理論</u>、<u>マーケティング</u>、<u>統計学</u>のコア・カリキュラムに加えて、各グループの科目から、1つ選んでください。

<u>グループ 1</u>	<u>グループ 2</u>
法人権	国際法
情報工学	海事法
マスメディア	環境法
広報	契約法

さらに情報が必要な方は、我々のホームページ <u>http://smarbusac.com</u> をご覧ください。案内書・申込書が必要な方は、<u>info@smarbusac.com</u> へメールか、イギリス

EPL 978 エバープール・エッジヒル・スマートビジネスアカデミーまでお手紙にてお問い合わせください。

宛先　　info@smarbusac.com
送信者　K. Izumi <ki@yamail.co.jp>
件名　　ビジネス＆法律の資格免許

スマート・ビジネス・アカデミー様

ウィークリー・インターナショナルの広告を拝見し、上記のコースに登録したいと思っておりますが、いくつかお伺いしたいことがあります。

国際法と海事法を両方受講することは可能でしょうか。それともどちらか一つを選ばなければならないでしょうか。私は大手国際海運会社の従業員で、会社が6ヶ月間のコースを受講する時間と費用を保証してくれるとのことなので、そのようなコースを受講したいと思っております。ビジネスと法律という二つの異なったクラスは、我社そして私自身に密接に関係しています。ゆえに、可能であれば両方勉強させていただきたく思います。また、経理の高度な国家資格を持っているのですが、それはそちらのビジネス＆法理コースの資格よりレベルが高いと思われますので、経理のコースを免除していただき、代わりにグループ1からもう一つ余分に授業を取るということはできないでしょうか。情報工学を受講したいと思っておりますが、法人権の授業も加えて受講させていただけるとたいへんうれしく思います。

以上、よろしくお願いいたします。

敬具
泉邦夫

Q1 この6ヶ月間の集中講座を修了すると、どうなりますか。
　（A）経営学修士号が受け取れる。
　（B）経営管理者にならなくてはならない。
　（C）経営学修士プログラムに応募できる。
　（D）経営学修士号を授与される。

Q2 どの学生がこの集中講座を修了できますか。
(A) 経理、経営理論、マーケティング、統計学、マスメディア、広報を修了した学生
(B) 経営理論、マーケティング、統計学、マスメディア、国際法を修了した学生
(C) 経理、経営理論、統計学、法人権、契約法を修了した学生
(D) 経理、経営理論、マーケティング、統計学、マスメディア、海事法を修了した学生

Q3 泉氏の職業はおそらく何ですか。
(A) 彼はビジネス専攻の学生である。
(B) 彼は会社の雇い主である。
(C) 彼は企業の従業員である。
(D) 彼は教育機関の弁護士である。

Q4 泉氏はメールでいくつの質問をしましたか。
(A) 1つ
(B) 2つ
(C) 3つ
(D) 4つ

Q5 泉氏はなぜ経理の授業を免除してもらえるかどうかを知りたいのですか。
(A) グループ1のコースをもっと取りたいから。
(B) すでに経理の資格を持っているから。
(C) より高いレベルの経理のコースを取りたいから。
(D) 情報工学のコースを選ぶつもりだから。

解答・解説 answer and explanation

Answer 1 (C)
広告に Successful completion of the Diploma in Business & Law will entitle candidates for the M.B.A. course とあり、経営学修士コースを受講する資格が与えられるのだから、(C) が正解である。

Answer 2 (D)
コア・カリキュラムである「経理、経営理論、マーケティング、統計学」は必ず受講しなくてはならず、グループ1と2から1つずつ選択しなければならないのだから、正解は (D) である。

Answer 3 (C)

電子メールに I am employed by a large international shipping corporation, とあるので、(C) が正解である。

Answer 4 (B)

電子メールの中で、「国際法と海事法を両方受講してよいか、それとも1つを選ばなくてはならないのか」という質問と、「すでに経理の国家資格を持っているので、経理のクラスは免除してもらい別のクラスを受講できるか」という2つの質問をしているので、正解は (B) である。

Answer 5 (B)

電子メールに I hold a National Certificate in Accountancy, which I believe is of a higher level than the accountancy module in your Diploma in Business & the Law course, とあり、「自分はすでに、スマート・ビジネス・アカデミーで開講されている経理のコースよりレベルが高いと思われる経理の国家資格を持っている」とあるので、(B) が正解である。

覚えてトクする語彙

diplomatic 形 外交の、外交辞令的な ★★★
diplomacy 名 外交 ★★★
diplomat 名 外交官 ★★★
extensive 形 広範囲にわたる ★★★
incentive 名 奨励（金）、動機・刺激 ★★★
innovation 名 革新 ★★★
entitlement 名 資格、権利 ★★★
equivalence 名 同等 ★★★
enrollment 名 入学、入会 ★★★
certification 名 証明、免許 ★★★
certify 動 …を証明する ★★★
take ~ for granted 形 …を当然のことと思う ★★★
exemption 名 免除、免税 ★★★
administration 名 経営、管理、政府 ★★★
administer 動 …を管理する ★★★
administrative 形 管理の、行政の ★★★
Academy Award 名 アカデミー賞 ★★★
qualify 動 （…の）資格を得る 《for, to *do*》 ★★★
qualified 形 資格がある ★★★

Questions 1 to 5 refer to the following e-mail and agreement.

To: IT related company
From: The Committee of the Annual Information Technology Trade Fair
Subject: The third Annual Information Technology Trade Fair

Dear Friends,

We are staging the third Annual Information Technology Trade Fair at the Empire Convention Center in San Francisco from October 10 to 12. You are invited to exhibit at the trade fair.

Our second trade fair last year was, by any measure, an unmitigated success with the attendance of more than 1,000 companies including 80 exhibitors and 50 representatives of the press, which had 50% more attendees than the first fair! We expect that the three-day event this year will bring over 1,500 of the world's top IT companies.

Last year, the booth space was sold out a month before the trade fair. We recommend that you make arrangements for your booth today! Booth space is available on a first-come-first-served basis. Apply now to secure the space you would prefer! To reserve your space, read the attached exhibit agreement, and complete the Exhibit Application with your choice of booth space and size.

All booths are provided with cable Internet and two telephone connections. Fees for Internet service provision are included in the exhibitors fees. Payment for telephone and facsimile service depends on use. You will receive confirmation of your booth number and an Exhibitor Kit within three weeks after submitting your application.

For more detailed information about our annual trade fair including booth rates, visit www.ittradefair.com. We hope you can join us in our third fair. Don't delay! Apply today!

Exhibit Agreement

* All devices which interfere with other electronic devices are prohibited.
* Exhibitors will be held fully responsible for any loss or damage to the exhibition premises, facilities or exhibition materials caused by the exhibitor and will be held liable for full and timely compensation in the event of such losses and damages.
* On termination of the period for which the agreement has been made the exhibitor will undertake to remove all items which were not supplied by the conference organizer in the shortest reasonable time and to leave the exhibition area as clean and tidy as at the start of the agreement.

Q1 What is this mail for?
　　(A) To invite the writer's friends to the trade fair
　　(B) To notify the exhibit agreement to the exhibitors
　　(C) To report the last year's trade fair
　　(D) To call for volunteers of the exhibitions

Q2 How was the trade fair last year?
　　(A) It was very successful.
　　(B) It was as successful as the first fair.
　　(C) It was not successful at all.
　　(D) It was less successful than expected.

Q3 What does an exhibitor NOT have to do?
 (A) To accept the exhibit agreement
 (B) To fill out the application form
 (C) To specify the booth space and size
 (D) To request cables for Internet

Q4 What is NOT included in the exhibitors fees?
 (A) Internet service
 (B) Telephone expenses
 (C) Facsimile connections
 (D) An Exhibitor Kit

Q5 What is banned?
 (A) To use electronic devices
 (B) To compensate for any loss and damage
 (C) To arrange the exhibition area
 (D) To remove all items in the booth

《語彙のヒント》

IT 图 情報工学、情報通信技術（= information technology） ★★★
[aití:]

trade fair 图 (産業) 見本市 ★★★
[tréid fèər]

by any measure 形 どのような基準に照らしても ★★★
[bai əni méʒər]

unmitigated 形 軽減されていない ★★★
[ʌnmítəgeitid]

press 图 報道機関、(新聞・雑誌) 記者 ★★★
[prés]

booth 图 (展示会の) 展示スペース、ブース (小さく仕切った部屋) ★★★
[bú:θ]

first-come-first-served basis 名 先着順 ★★★
[fə́ːrstkʌ́mfəːrstsə́ːrvd bèisis]

provision 名 用意、対策 ★★★
[prəvíʒən]

confirmation 名 確認 ★★★
[kànfərméiʃən]

kit 名 (道具・教材などの) 1セット、ひとそろい、(道具一式用の) 箱 ★★★
[kít]

submit 動 …を提出する、(人)を服従させる ★★★
[səbmít]

device 名 装置、道具 ★★★
[diváis]

interfere 動 (…を) 妨げる《with》 ★★★
[ìntərfíər]

prohibit 動 (法律などが) …を禁止する ★★★
[prouhíbit]

premise 名 構内、店舗、前提 ★★★
[prémis]

facility 名 (複数形で) 設備、施設 ★★★
[fəsíləti]

liable 名 法的責任がある、…しがちな《to do》 ★★★
[láiəbl]

compensation 名 賠償・補償金 ★★★
[kàmpənséiʃən]

termination 名 終了 ★★★
[tə̀ːrmənéiʃən]

tidy 形 きちんとした ★★★
[táidi]

ban 動 …を (法律で) 禁止する 名 禁止 (令) ★★★
[bǽn]

第3章 ● パート7 読解問題（2つの文書）

日本語訳

質問1～5は次の電子メールと同意書に関するものです。

宛先：IT関連会社
送信者：情報通信技術見本市年次大会委員会
件名：第3回情報通信見本市年次大会

皆様

　10月10日から12日まで、サンフランシスコのエンパイア・コンベンション・センターにおいて、第3回情報通信技術見本市年次大会を行います。見本市での展示を募集しています。

　昨年の第2回見本市では、80の展示社を含む1,000社以上と報道関係者50人が参加し、これは第1回見本市の50％増で、どう少なく見積もりましても、大成功を収めた次第です。今年の3日間のイベントでは、世界でもトップクラスのIT企業1,500社を見込んでおります。

　昨年は、展示スペースが見本市の1ヶ月前に、いっぱいとなってしまいましたので、今日すぐにでも展示スペースの予約をお勧めいたします。展示スペースは先着順で決定させていただきます。よりよい展示スペースを確保できるよう、すぐにお申し込みください。展示スペースの予約をするには、添付した展示同意書をお読みください。そして展示スペースのブースの場所とサイズを選択の上、申込書をご記入ください。

　すべてのブースには、インターネットケーブルと電話線2本が備え付けられています。インターネットサービスの費用は、展示費用に含まれております。電話・ファックス代は、使用料金をお支払い願います。申込書を提出していただいてから3週間以内に、ブース番号の確認と展示用品セットが届きます。

　ブースの料金を含めました見本市年次大会について詳細をお求めの方は、www.ittradefair.comにてご確認ください。第3回見本市でお目にかかることを願っております。遅くならないうちに、今すぐお申し込みください。

展示同意書

* 電子機器を妨げるすべての機器の使用は禁止されています。
* 展示スペースに備えられたファックスや展示資料などの損失については、すべて展示者側の責任で補償していただきます。
* 契約にある期間終了後、あらかじめ備え付けられていた以外のすべての物は速やかに撤去し、展示スペースを清潔にきちんと使用前の状態にしてください。

Q1 このメールの目的は何ですか
　(A) 筆者の友達を見本市に招くため
　(B) 展示する人に展示同意を知らせるため
　(C) 昨年度の見本市について報告するため
　(D) 展示の志願者を募るため

Q2 昨年度の見本市はどうでしたか。
　(A) 大成功だった。
　(B) 第1回と同じくらい成功した。
　(C) 失敗した。
　(D) 期待はずれだった。

Q3 展示する人がしなくてもよいことは何ですか。
　(A) 展示同意書の内容を受け入れる
　(B) 申込書に記入する
　(C) ブースの場所とサイズを特定する
　(D) インターネットケーブルを要求する

Q4 展示料金に含まれていないものはどれですか。
　(A) インターネットサービス
　(B) 電話代
　(C) ファックス接続
　(D) 展示用品セット

Q5 禁止されているのは何ですか。
　(A) 電子機器の使用
　(B) 損失の補償
　(C) 展示スペースのアレンジ
　(D) ブースのすべての物の撤去

解答・解説

answer and explanation

Answer 1　(D)

メールに You are invited to exhibit at the trade fair. とあり、そのための情報が情報が書かれているので、正解は (D) である。

Answer 2 　　　　　　　　　　　　　　　　　　　　　　　　　　　　　　(A)
Our second trade fair last year was, by any measure, an unmitigated success とあるので、「どのような基準に照らし合わせても、軽減のない成功だった」ということから、成功だったことがわかる。また、第1回と比べてみても、参加者が50％増しだったということから、正解は（A）である。

Answer 3 　　　　　　　　　　　　　　　　　　　　　　　　　　　　　　(D)
メールに All booths are provided with cable Internet とあるので、すべてのブースにインターネットケーブルはついていることがわかり、正解は（D）となる。

Answer 4 　　　　　　　　　　　　　　　　　　　　　　　　　　　　　　(B)
メールに Payment for telephone and facsimile service depends on use. とあるので、電話代やファックス代は展示者側持ちだということがわかり、正解は（B）である。

Answer 5 　　　　　　　　　　　　　　　　　　　　　　　　　　　　　　(D)
(A) の電子機器は、他の電子機器を妨げさえしなければ使えるので禁止されているわけではないので当てはまらない。ブースに持ち込んだものはすべて撤去しなければならないが、あらかじめ備え付けられていたものは元の状態にして置いておかなければならないので、正解は（D）である。あらかじめ備え付けられていたインターネットケーブルなどすべて持っていってしまうことは許されていない。

覚えてトクする語彙

mitigate 動 …を軽減する ★★★
mitigation 名 緩和、沈静 ★★★
press conference 名 記者会見 ★★★
provisional 形 仮の、暫定的な ★★★
confirm 動 …を確認する ★★★
submission 名 提出、服従 ★★★
submissive 形 服従的な ★★★
safety device 名 安全装置 ★★★
devise 動 …を考案する ★★★
interference 名 妨害、干渉 ★★★
prohibition 名 禁止 ★★★
liability 名 （補償などの）責任 ★★★
compensate 動 （人）に補償・賠償をする ★★★
terminate 動 …を終了させる ★★★
terminal 名 （鉄道・バス・飛行機などの）終点（始点）　形 最後の、終点（始点）の ★★★
terminal care 名 末期医療 ★★★

Questions 1 to 5 refer to the following e-mail and attachment.

To: M. H. Poirot
From: Koji Ueshima
Subject: Japanese representation for your products

Dear Mr. Poirot,

We have seen your company's name and advertisements in various Belgian periodicals and note that you are a major high quality glassware maker. Though undoubtedly priced at the high end of the market, each of your products is made by hand, and we are impressed by the quality. We understand that your workers endure years of hands-on training in order to become a craftsman.

Since there is an increasing demand in our sales area for imported high quality glassware in Japan, we are particularly keen to find a well-known manufacturer of the highest quality glassware who is willing to offer us a sole agency to retail their glassware in Japan. Since 1971, our company has been a high quality goods import agent, and already the sole agent for a major American, British, Italian, and French manufacturers of their high quality products.

We attach brief information about our company for your inspection. In case you need to know more about us, please check our website at www.tokyoimport.com Awaiting your answer to this mail with great interest.

Sincerely,
Koji Ueshima

Business Profile: Tokyo Import Trading Co.

Location: Corporate headquarters in Tokyo, branches in America, Britain, China, France, Germany, Italy and Korea

Business: Import of high quality furniture, home ornaments, glassware, pottery, cutlery, and many other luxurious home products. Dealing with more than fifty major manufacturers in twelve countries.

Employees: 350 worldwide with 150 based in Japan

Capital: 5.5billion U.S. dollars

Sales: Tokyo Import Co. had $1.8 million in annual sales last year. Since then, sales have increased about 150 % to over $2.9 million. Imported goods sales increase for the coming year is expected to be 20 % higher than this year.

Background: Founded in 1971 as a small individual importer. Tokyo Import has always concentrated on meeting the needs of a high-end niche market. We have never compromise our business philosophy of "Only The Very Best."

Future: To maintain and expand our position as the leader in importing fine home goods, Tokyo Import focuses on being a world-class importer of high quality luxurious home products and on increasing annual growth by at least 15 % each year.

Q1 What is the purpose of the mail?
- (A) To advertise in Belgian periodicals
- (B) To order some high quality glassware
- (C) To ask for some discount on fine glassware
- (D) To make a partnership agreement

Q2 Why is Poirot's glassware very expensive?
- (A) They advertise in various Belgian periodicals.
- (B) They sell their goods to U.S. at high prices.
- (C) Their products are made by adept artisans.
- (D) Their craftsmen require high salary.

Q3 What does Tokyo Import Co. most likely import?
- (A) Sleazy vase
- (B) Forgery painting
- (C) Luxurious coffin
- (D) Antique basin

Q4 In how many countries does Tokyo Import Co. have branches?
- (A) 4
- (B) 7
- (C) 12
- (D) 50

Q5 What percentage increase of sales is predicted for the next year?
- (A) 15%
- (B) 20%
- (C) 50%
- (D) 150%

語彙のヒント

Belgian 形 ベルギー(人)の 名 ベルギー人 ★★★
[béldʒən]

periodical 名 定期刊行物、雑誌 ★★★
[pìəriádikəl]

ornament 名 装飾品 ★★★
[ɔ́ːrnəmənt]

hands-on 形 実際的な、実用向きの ★★★
[hǽndzɔ́n]

craftsman 名 職人、熟練工 ★★★
[krǽftmən]

keen 形 機敏な、熱心な ★★★
[kíːn]

inspection 名 調査、検査 ★★★
[inspékʃən]

await 動 …を待つ (wait for よりも堅い語) ★★★
[əwéit]

branch 名 支店、枝 ★★★
[brǽntʃ]

pottery 名 陶器 ★★★
[pátəri]

cutlery 名 (ナイフ・スプーン・フォークなどの) 食事用器具 ★★★
[kʌ́tləri]

concentrate 動 (…に) 努力を集中する《on, upon》 ★★★
[kánsəntrèit]

niche 名 適した仕事 ★★★
[nítʃ]

compromise 動 …を妥協する 名 妥協 ★★★
[kámprəmàiz]

philosophy 名 哲学 ★★★
[filásəfi]

adept 形 熟練した《in, at》 ★★★
[ədépt]

artisan 名 職人 ★★★
[áːrtəzən]

sleazy 名 安っぽい ★★★
[slíːzi]

vase 名 花瓶 ★★★
[véis]

forgery 名 贋作、偽造品 ★★★
[fɔ́:rdʒəri]

coffin 名 棺 ★★★
[kɔ́:fin]

antique 形 骨董の、年代ものの 名 骨董品 ★★★
[æntí:k]

basin 名 水ばち、水盤 ★★★
[béisn]

predict 動 …を予測する、予言する ★★★
[pridíkt]

日本語訳　　translation

質問1～5は次の電子メールと添付ファイルによるものです。

宛先：M. H. ポワロ
送信者：上島孝司
件名：貴社製品に関して日本の代表者より

ポワロ様

私どもは貴社のお名前や宣伝をさまざまなベルギーの雑誌で拝見し、貴社は高品質のガラス製品の一流メーカーだと拝察いたしております。貴社製品は確かに高価ではありますが、すべて手作りで、我々はその品質の高さに感心しております。貴社の職員は熟練工になるため、何年もの現場訓練を重ねておられると、お察し申し上げます。

日本において高品質の輸入ガラス製品の需要が高まってきており、ガラス製品の小売りの単独取次店になっていただける最高品質のガラス製品有名会社を切望しております。弊社は、1971年以来、高品質の輸入品取次業をしており、すでにアメリカ・イギリス・イタリア・フランスの主なメーカーと、単独取次の契約を結んでおります。

弊社の簡単な情報を添付させていただきますので、ご査証ください。弊社に関しての詳細が必要な場合は、ホームページがございますので、www.tokyoimport.com をご覧ください。お返事をお待ちしております。

敬具
上島孝司

企業プロフィール：東京輸入貿易会社

事業所：本社東京。アメリカ、イギリス、中国、フランス、ドイツ、イタリア、韓国に支社。

事業内容：高品質の家具、家の装飾品、ガラス製品、陶器、食卓用金物、その他多くの贅沢な家庭用品の輸入。12カ国の50以上の製造会社と取引がある。

社員数：日本に150人。全世界で350人。

資本金：55億ドル。

売上：昨年の年間売上高は180万ドル。それ以来、売上は150％増の290万ドルと伸びている。来年の輸入品の売上高は、今年の20％増を見込んでいる。

沿革：1971年に、小さな個人輸入業者として設立。東京輸入貿易会社は、常に市場最高の要求に応えるべく努力している。「最高のものだけ」という企業哲学には決して妥協しない。

今後の展望：すばらしい家庭用品の輸入業のリーダーとしての地位を保持し広げるため、東京輸入貿易会社は、最高品質の贅沢な家庭用品の世界レベルでの輸入と、毎年少なくとも15％の年間売上増加を重点目標に掲げている。

Q1 このメールの目的は何ですか。
　(A) ベルギーの雑誌に宣伝するため
　(B) 高品質のガラス製品を輸入するため
　(C) すばらしいガラス製品を安くしてもらうため
　(D) 提携の同意を得るため

Q2 ポワロのガラス製品が非常に高価なのはなぜですか。
　(A) さまざまなベルギーの雑誌に広告を載せているから。
　(B) 製品をアメリカに高価格で売っているから。
　(C) 熟練工によって製品が作られているから。
　(D) 熟練工が高い給料を要求するから。

Q3 東京輸入貿易会社は、おそらくどの品物を輸入していますか。
　(A) 安っぽい花瓶
　(B) 絵画の贋作
　(C) 贅沢な棺
　(D) 骨董の水盤

Q4 東京輸入貿易会社は、何カ国に支社がありますか。
 (A) 4
 (B) 7
 (C) 12
 (D) 50

Q5 来年の売上増加は何パーセントと予想されていますか。
 (A) 15％
 (B) 20％
 (C) 50％
 (D) 150％

解答・解説 answer and explanation

Answer 1 (D)
メール文中に we are particularly keen to find a well-known manufacturer of the highest quality glassware who is willing to offer us a sole agency to retail their glassware in Japan. とあり、自分たちに独占的に販売権を与えてくれるような高品質のガラス製品製造業者を探していることがわかる。よって、正解は「提携を結びたい」という (D) である。

Answer 2 (C)
メール文中に Though undoubtedly priced at the high end of the market, と、「価格は疑いなく市場でももっとも高い」と値段が高いことを示したすぐ後に、「品質を考えると納得がいく」とあり、さらにそれに続けて「品質が高いのは、熟練工によるものだ」とあるので、正解は (C) である。

Answer 3 (D)
事業内容のところに、Import of high quality furniture, home ornament, glassware, pottery, cutlery, and other luxurious home products. とあるので、(D) が正解である。(C) の棺は家庭用品ではない。

Answer 4 (B)
事業所のところに、branches in America, Britain, China, France, Germany, Italy and Korea とあるので、支社は7ヶ国であることがわかる。よって、正解は (B) になる。

Answer 5 (B)
売上のところに Imported goods sales increase for the coming year is expected to be 20 ％ higher than this year. とあり、「今年より 20 ％の増加を期待している」とあるので、正解は (B) である。

覚えてトクする語彙

Belgium 图 ベルギー ★★★
hands-off 形 無干渉の ★★★
hands-free 形 手を使わずに操作できる ★★★
craft 图 (手の技術を必要とする) 仕事、工芸、飛行機、船舶 ★★★
keenly 副 強烈に、熱心に、鋭敏に ★★★
inspect 動 …を調査する、検査する ★★★
inspector 图 調査官、検閲官 ★★★
porcelain 图 磁器 ★★★
lacquer ware 图 漆器 ★★★
concentration 图 集中 ★★★
prediction 图 予測、予言 ★★★
predictable 形 予測できる ★★★
unpredictable 形 予測できない ★★★

索 引

A

a cut above ~	91
a dime a dozen	37
a staff member	168
a world of difference	67
Academy Award	206
accept	168
acceptability	168
acceptable	168
acceptance	168
acceptant	168
accepted	168
acclaim	202
accommodate	64
accommodating	65
accommodation	65
accommodator	65
account	16, 65
account number	65
account records	65
accountability	17
accountable	17
accountancy	202
accountant	65
accounting	64
accounting department	65
accounting manager	65
accuracy	158
accurate	156
achievement	27
acidophilus milk	171
adept	217
adhere	123
adherent	123
adhesive	121
adhesive bandage	123
administer	206
administration	206
administrative	206
administrator	203
admission	193
admit	197
admittance	197
advance	35
advanced	34
advancement	35
affection	13
affectionate	13
against the clock	61
agrichemical	75
agriculture	75
aid	94
aide	95
aim	62
aimless	63
air cargo	33
air conditioner	33
Air Force	33
Air Force One	33
air turbulence	33
aircraft	32
airfare	33
airfreight	33
airhead	33
airlift	33
airtight	33
alarm clock	39
alarming	39
alias	143
allergen	153
allergic	153
allergist	153
allergy	151
amenity	38
anesthetist	13
annual revenue	113
annual turnover	73
annually	73
antihistamine	153
antique	218
apologize	130
apology	131
appearance	95
applicable	25, 143
application	25
application deadline	135
application form	25
applied	25
apply	25
approvable	158
approval	156
approve	158
approved	158

approver	158
approving	158
arranged marriage	31, 131
arrangement	130
arrangements	31
arsenic	193
artificial	106
artificial intelligence	107
artificial respiration	107
artificiality	107
artisan	217
as a last resort	39
as a result	138
as of	185
assumable	13
assumably	13
assume	12
assuming	13
assumption	13
at any price	11
(at) first hand	77
at issue	81
attach	193
attachment	197
attend	54
ATTN	134
autograph	111
automobile	83
average	68, 102
await	217
award	203

B

ballot	88
ban	210
bank account	101
bank book	101
bank note	101
bank statement	101
bank teller	100
bank [count] on ~	55
banker	55
banking	54
bankroll	55
bankrupt	53
bankruptcy	52
bar graph	163
basin	218
be cut out for ~	91

be cut up	91
be dead set against ~	61
be in need of ~	95
be in position	47
be on cloud nine	49
be out of position	47
be overrun with ~	167
bean curd	181
beat	180
beat *one's* head against a wall	61
bed wetting	65
bedding	64
beer belly	69
Belgian	217
Belgium	219
belittle	47
berry	181
between *one's* teeth	95
between ourselves	95
bewitch	47
bifidus	171
billion	121
billionaire	105
blackberry	179
blame	74
blameful	75
blameless	75
blizzard	49
block	151
blockade	153
blue chips	15
bond	14
bond certificate	15
boost	102
booster	103
booth	209
box number	145
branch	217
breast cancer	49
brew	23, 69
brewer	69
brewery	22, 69
brief	39
briefcase	39
briefing	39
briefly	38
bring the house down	63
brochure	193
build up ~	81
bunk bed	65

burglar alarm	39
burn	86
burn a hole in *one's* pocket	87
burn *one's* fingers	87
burn the midnight oil	87
burn up the road	87
burned-out	87
burner	87
business-to-business	138
by all means	19
by any means	19
by any measure	209
by means of ~	19
by no means	19

C

cancer	48
cancerous	49
candid	9
Candid Camera	9
candidate	8
capital assets	59
capital gains	59
capital punishment	59
capitalize	59
capitalize on ~	59
carbon chloride	193
carbon dioxide	198
carrier	185
cash	101
cash in on ~	101
cashier	100
cast	88
caution	171
cautionary	173
cautious	173
cautiousness	173
CEO	92
certificate	203
certification	206
certify	206
chairman	92
checkup	23
chief	93
Chief Executive Officer	55
chimney sweep	27
chip	104
choose	9
circumference	93

circumlocution	93
circumscribe	93
circumspect	93
circumvent	93
claim	66
clear	161
cloudless	49
cloudy	48
coffin	218
comb	39
combination	39
combine	38
combined pollution	39
combo	39
come about	81
come across ~	81
come by ~	81
come down with ~	81
come from behind	81
come in for ~	81
come in handy	77
come into ~	81
come into effect	13
come into *one's* own	23
come over	81
come to	81
come to *one's* senses	81
come up	80
command	45
commandant	45
commandeer	45
commander	45
commandment	45
commission	198
commissioner	194
commit	9
commitment	9
committee	8
communicate	41
communication	41
communication gap	41
communications	41
communications satellite	40
communism	79
compensate	213
compensation	210
component	202
comprise	62
compromise	217
computerize	99

computerized	98
concentrate	217
concentration	219
conference	193
conference call	127
conference hall	125
confidence	70
confident	71
confidential	71
confidentially	71
confiding	71
confirm	213
confirmation	210
conjunct	177
conjunction	175
conjunctive	177
consider	138
considerable	139
considerate	139
consideration	139
considering	139
consistency	27
consistent	26
constant	61
constantly	60
consumable	11
consume	11
consumedly	11
consumer	10
consumer price index	11
consumption	11
consumption tax	11
continual	41
continuation	41
continue	40
continuity	41
continuous	41
continuum	41
contraband	168
contraception	168
contract	30
contraction	31
contractor	194
contradict	168
contradiction	168
contradictory	167
contrary	89
contrast	88
contrastive	89
contravene	168

copier	33
copy	32
corporate bonds	15
corporation tax	45
correspond	145
correspondence	145
correspondent	145
corresponding	143
corrupt	42
corruption	43
counsel	44
countercharge	69
counterfeit	69
countersign	69
cover letter	24
cover story	25
craft	219
craftsman	217
creation	115
creative	115
creativity	115
credence	139
credential	138
credibility	51
credible	51
credit	50
credit card	51
credit line	51
credit union	51
creditability	51
creditable	51
creditor	51
crisis management	55
crop	36
crop circle	37
crop up	37
curd	179
current account	160
curriculum vitae	24
custom	185
customer service	130
customs	161
customs-cleared	160
cut a figure	91
cut corners	91
cut down on ~	91
cut loose	91
cut no ice	91
cutlery	217

D

daily	94
debtor	51
decor	69
decorate	68
decoration	69
decorative	69
delinquency	145
delinquent	143
Democratic Party	109
dental checkup	23
dependability	135
depress	99
depressed	21, 99
depressing	99
depression	20, 98
dermatologist	13
designed	115
designer	115
designer label	115
designing	115
determination	91
determine	90
determined	91
deterrence	158
deterrent	156
developing country	35
device	210
devise	213
die hard	87
die in the saddle	87
die [wither] on the vine	87
diet	25
Diet	25
dietary	24
dime	37
dioxin	194
diploma	202
diplomacy	206
diplomat	206
diplomatic	206
diplomatic representative	43
direct	93
director	92
directory	76
disaster	74
disastrous	75
disburse	21
discomfit	21
discontinue	41
disintegrate	20
dismiss	14
dismissal	15
dismount	21
disown	21
dispatch	30
displace	70
displacement	71
disposable	197
disposal	193
dispose	197
dissolution	45
dissolve	44
distillery	23
distribute	11
distribution	11
distributor	10
divergence	51
divergent	51
diversion	51
divide	31
dividend	31
division	31
divulgence	51
document	52
domestic revenue	113
down payment	43
download	147
downplay	43
downpour	43
downright	42
downsize	43
downsized	43
downturn	43
draft	72
draft beer	69
drafty	73
dramatic	35
drastic	34
draw a blank	158
draw near	158
draw on ~	158
draw the curtain over [on] ~	158
draw up ~	156
drive	48
driver's license	41
drought	74
droughty	75
due to ~	129

duty	133
dwindle	46

E

earn	103
earned income	103
earner	103
earning	103
earnings	11, 102
ecological	198
ecology	193
economic indicator	29
economic stimulus measures	29
edition	32
effect	185
effective	188
elect	89
elective	89
electric	89
electricity	89
electrocardiogram	89
electron	89
electronic	88, 121
electronic mail	89
electronics	89, 123
embezzle	101
embezzlement	100
emergence	177
emergency	177
emergent	177
emission	194
emit	198
emphasis	108
emphasize	109
emphatic	109
encode	71
encumber	71
endear	71
endow	71
engulf	70
enjoin	71
enroll	202
enrollment	206
entirely	31
entitle	202
entitlement	206
entrench	71
entrepreneur	194
entry	133

entry fee	135
entry visa	135
entryway	135
environ	71
envisage	71
equivalence	206
equivalent	202
establishment	77
estate	55
estate tax	55
estimative	57
estimator	57
evacuate	38
evacuation	39
excel	59
excellence	59
excellent	58
excite	91
excitement	91
execute	55, 177
execution	55, 175
executive	54, 93
executive board	55
executive committee	55
exempt	203
exemption	206
exhibit	96
exhibition	97
exhibitive	97
exhibitor	97
expect	83
expectancy	83
expectant	83
expectation	82
expedite	185
expedition	188
expiration	143
expire	145
explicit	31
expose	82
exposition	83
expository	83
exposure	83
extensive	206
external	53
external medicine	53
external pressure	53
externality	53
externalization	53
externalize	53

F

fabric conditioner	107
facility	210
fade	14
fade in	15
fade out	15
fair	29
fair and square	29
fair to middling	29
fair-haired	29
fair-weather	29
false	38
false alarm	39
false praise	39
fare	28, 62
farewell	29
farm	37
farmer	36
farmfresh vegetables	37
farming	37
fault	149
fault finding	149
faultless	149
faulty	147
feel blue	67
feel cheap	67
feel for ~	67
feel free to ~	67
feel ~ in *one's* bones	67
feel like a million dollars	67
ferment	171
fermentable	173
fermentation	173
few and far between	101
fidelity	72
filling	180
finance	54
finance company	55
financier	55
fingerprint	121
fingertip	123
firm	76
first and foremost	91
first-come-first-served basis	210
fiscal year	104
five-star hotel	71
flexibility	135
flexible	133
flextime	135
flier	62
flight	94
flight number	95
flight path	95
flight recorder	95
flurry	49
fly	63
fly off the handle	63
fly the coop	63
fold	181
folded refrigerated unbaked piecrust	179
follow in *a person's* footsteps	158
follow *one's* nose	158
follow suit to ~	158
follow up ~	156
food processor	19
for (all) the world	67
for or against ~	61
forecast	104
foremost	91
foresee	105
foreseeable	105
forgery	218
foundation	77
founder	77
four-alarm fire	70
fraud	16
frequency	67
frequent	67
frequent flyer	67
frequently	66
fright	95
fry	63
function	18
functional	19
fund	73
fund raiser	74
funding	73
fund-raising	75

G

gain	28
gain ground	29
gaining issues	15
garment	194
gastric cancer	49
gastroenteritis	173
gastroenterology	171
gastrointestinal	173

gastrology	173
gauge	28
generic	156
get a handle on ~	21
give *a person* credit for ~	51
give the world to do	67
global	102
global warming	103
globalism	103
globalize	103
globe	103
gloom	20
gloomy	21
go against the [*one's*] grain with ~	61
go ahead	129
go [into] bankruptcy	53
government bonds	15
Govt.	109
grant	203
grinded meat	19
grownup	37
guarantee	171
guidance	33
guideline	33
gynecologist	13

H

hand over fist	33
handicap	83
handicapped	82
handle	64
handout	77
hands-free	219
hands-off	219
hands-on	217
have *one's* head in the clouds	49
have *one's* own way	23
have two strikes against one	61
hazard	82
hazardous	83
headline	56
headlong	57
headquarters	57, 90
high-tech	121
histamine	151
hit it off	79
hit on ~	79
hit *one's* sore spot	79
hit the books	79

hit the ceiling	79
hit the hay [sack]	79
hit the jackpot	79
hit the road	79
hit the spot	79
hold *one's* own	23
hold over ~	33
home economics	37
homemade	37
homemaker	37
household	62, 106
household goods	63
householder	63, 107
housekeeper	107
housekeeping	107
housemaker	107
housework	107
housing	63
housing complex	63
hrs	133
human resources	12, 134
human resources development	135

I

identical	99
identifiable	123
identification	121
identification card	99
if need be	95
imminence	97
imminent	96
impede	106
impediment	107
implant	12
implantation	13
implement	114
implementation	115
implication	31
implicit	31
imply	30
impress	138
impression	139
impressive	139
improve	83
improvement	82
in a sense	81
in advance	35
in appearance	95
in brief	39

229

in effect	13
in principle	95
Inc.	50
incentive	206
incinerate	198
incineration	194
incinerator	198
inconvenience	130
inconvenient	131
indispensable	58
individualism	99
individualist	99
individuality	99
individualize	99
indoor	69
industrial waste water	35
industrialism	35
industrialist	35
industrialize	35
inflate	27
inflation	26
inflationary	27
inflationary spiral	27
in-house	69
in-house training	69
innovation	206
innovative	202
in-room	68
insist	185
insistence	188
insistent	188
inspect	219
inspection	217
inspector	219
insurant	17
insurer	17
intensive	202
intentionally	111
interfere	210
interference	213
internal audit	53
internal medicine	53
internal organs	53
international revenue	113
invest	73
investment	72
investor	73
invoice	185
irrelevance	115
irrelevant	115
issue	80
IT	209
itchy	151
item	46
itemize	47

J

job candidate	9
judge	14
judgment	15
judgmental	15
judicial	15
judicious	15
juridical counselor	45
juvenile delinquency	145

K

keen	217
keenly	219
keep track of ~	27
key in ~	29
key money	29
keynote	29
keynote address	29
kit	210

L

lacquer ware	219
lager beer	69
land	84
land on *one's* feet	85
landfill	85, 194
landing	85
landlord	85
landmark	85
landmine	85
landowner	85
landscape	85
landslide	85
language	18
language laboratory	19
languid	19
languish	19
law firm	15
law school	15
law-abiding	109
lawbreaking	109

lawmaker	108
lawmaking	109
lawsuit	14
lay down the law	105
lay off ~	104
lay [stop] over	105
lay the groundwork for ~	105
L/C	78
lean against ~	61
legislate	87
legislation	87
legislature	86
lemon peel	180
letter of credit	111
letter opener	111
letterhead	111
liability	213
liable	210
license	41
license plate	41
licensing fees	41
life expectancy	83
lift a hand [finger]	21
line-graph	165
liquid	97
liquidate	97
liquidation	96
liquidator	97
liquidity	97
list price	11
litigate	15
litigation	15
live on [off] the fat of the land	85
live within *one's* means	19
lose	89
lose face	49
lose no time (in) doing	49
lose *one's* shirt	49
lose one's temper	49
lose sleep over [about]	49
loser	89
Ltd.	156
luscious	39
luxurious	39
luxury	38

M

mail box	149
mail order	147
mailing address	149
mail-order house	149
major in ~	75
majority	75
make a beeline for ~	79
make a fast buck	79
make a killing	79
make a name (for *oneself*)	79
make a splash	57
make a toast	79
make allowance(s) for ~	79
make do with ~	79
make good	57
make headway	57
make no bones about ~	79
make sense	57, 81
make the grade	57
make time	57
make waves	57
manage	55
manageable	55
management	55
manager	54
manufacture	106
manufacturer	107
maritime	202
market price	103
market research [survey]	103
market share	102
market value	103
marketable	103
market-driven	103
marketing	103
masking tape	121
mass communication	41
meat-and-potatoes	19
media	167
Medicaid	21
medical checkup	23
Medicare	21
medicate	21
medication	20
memoir	105
memorabilia	105
memorable	105
memorandum	125
memorial	105
memorization	105
memorize	105
mention	19

231

merchandise	160
merchandising	161
merchant	161
minimum wage	93
miscellaneous	163
miserable	151
misery	153
mission	74
missionary	75
mitigate	213
mitigation	213
mix A up with B	49
mixer	49
mixture	49
mix-up	49
model	129
model agency	131
moderate	26
moderately	27
moderation	27
moderator	27
module	202
mom-and-pop	50
money order	147
monitor	165
monitoring	163
monitory	165
monthly	95
more often than not	91
motor vehicle	60
mountainous	84
multi-factorial	57
multi-function	56
multilateral	57
multilingual	57
multi-national	57
multiple	57
multiple-choice	57
multi-purpose	57
multi-symptom	151
multivitamin	171
mutual	73
mutual fund	72
mutuality	73
mutually	73

N

nearby	29
nearsighted	29
negotiable	59, 93
negotiate	59, 92
negotiation	58, 93
negotiator	59, 93
net	104
niche	217
nickel	37
night shift	109
no more than	91
northbound	101
northern	101
northern hemisphere	101
northernmost	100
nose bleeding	151
not more than	91
not to mention ~	18
notice	9
notifiable	131
notification	131
notify	129
novice	175
numerous	82

O

object	95
objection	95
objective	94
occasion	44
occasional	45
occasionally	45
odor	193
of *one's* own accord	23
off *one's* own bat	23
off the record	37
offensive	193
officer	93
official	93
officially	93
on [the, an] average	69
on *one's* hands	77
on the back burner	87
on the charge of ~	17
on the contrary	89
on the house	63
on the increase	83
on the move	133
on top of the world	67
on-the-job	138
operate	89

operating revenue	113
operation	89
operational	89
operations department	125
operator	88
opportune	99
opportunism	99
opportunistic	99
opportunity	98
optical fiber	194
oral	30
orbit	40
orbital	41
ornament	217
out of hand	77
out of place	31
out of this [the] world	67
outdoor	69
outfit	11
outlay	11
outplacement	11
outright	11
outstanding	11
over and above	33
over and over again	33
over one's dead body	33
over the top	33
overall	80
overdose	111
overhaul	67
overhead	111
overissue	111
overpay	66
overproduction	111
override	67
overrun	111, 169
overseas	121
oversee	123
overseer	123
oversight	111
overtake	67
over-the-counter	156
overthrow	67
overtime	110
overuse	111
overview	111
overweight	111
own	23
owner	22
oz.	179

P

package	34
package tour	35
pan	180
pants	117
pass away	87
pass for ~	87
pass out	87
pass the buck to ~	87
pass up ~	87
pastry	180
payback	47
paycheck	46
payday	47
payment	47
payroll	47
pediatric	171
pediatrician	13, 173
pediatrics	173
peel	181
penny	37
pension	96
pensioner	97
per	59
per annum	59
per diem	59
perform	113
performance	112
performance appraisal	113
performance test	113
performance-related pay	113
periodical	217
permission	97
personal estate	55
personnel	138
petrochemical	194
petroleum	193
pharmaceutical	125, 194
pharmacist	127, 198
pharmacy	127, 198
philosophy	217
physician	13
pie chart	165
piecrust	181
pkg.	179
place	31
placebo	31
placement	31
placet	31

233

plant capacity	117
plant manager	117
plastic surgery	13
play it safe	83
plea	17
pleabargain	17
plead	16
plead guilty	17
porcelain	219
posit	47
post	88
post office box	143
post-communist	78
poster	89
potency	139
potent	139
potential	138
potentially	139
pottery	217
powdered sugar	179
predict	218
predictable	219
prediction	219
premise	210
presidential	44
presidential candidate	9
presidential election	45
presidential primary	45
press	116, 209
press agency	117
press briefing	117
press campaign	117
press clipping	117
press conference	117, 213
press kit	117
presumable	17
presumably	17
presumption	17
prevail	101
prevailing	101
prevalent	100
prevent	24
prevention	25
preventive	25
preventive medicine	25
price	10
priceless	11
prick	180
pricy	11
principal	95
principally	94
principle	95
probiotics	171
procedural	75
procedure	75
proceeding	75
process	19, 134
processed	135
processed food	135
procession	19, 75
processor	18
profit	91, 112
profitability	123
profitable	90, 121
profitably	123
profitless	91
progress	99
progress report	99
progression	75, 99
progressive	75, 98
prohibit	210
prohibition	213
project	8
projection	9
projective	9
projector	9
prompt	131
promptly	130
proposal	156
propose	158
proprietary	45
proprietary company	45
proprietary name	45
proprietor	45
proprietorship	44
prospectus	202
provided	97
provision	97, 210
provisional	213
public finance	55
public relations	169, 202
Public Relations Office	167
Puerto Rican	117
purpose	114
purposeful	115
purposeless	115
purposely	115

Q

quadruplets	113
qualification	203
qualified	206
qualify	206
quarter	11, 36, 112
quarterly	37
quartet	37
quintuplets	113
quite a few	101
quorum	27
quota	26, 43
quotable	43
quotation	27, 47
quote	27, 46

R

rank	58
rank and file	59
ranking	59
react	153
reaction	151
reactionary	153
read between the lines	95
real estate	54
rebel against ～	61
rebellion	85
rebellious	85
recall	20
reception	125
reception clerk	135
reception desk	127, 135
receptionist	127, 133
record	36
record holder	37
recover	107
reduce	193
reduction	197
reductive	198
refund	66
register	193
regret	30
regretful	31
regrettable	31
regulate	171
regulation	173
regulative	173
regulator	173
regulatory	173
relevance	115, 198
relevant	114, 193
remark	193
remarkable	198
remarkably	198
remediable	188
remedial	188
remedy	185
remissible	145
remission	145
remit	143
remittance	145
repair	110
repairman	111
replace	22, 31
replacement	23, 30
report	18
report card	19
reportedly	19
represent	43
representation	43
representative	42
Representative	43
reprimand	167
reprisal	85
Republican	108
Republican Party	109
reputable	77
reputation	76
require	65
requirement	65
requisite	65
research	34
research and development	35
researcher	35
respect	80
respectful	81
respective	81
respectively	81
restructure	117
restructuring	116
restructuring benefit	117
restructuring cost [charge]	117
restructuring plan	117
result from ～	139
result in ～	139
résumé	17, 134
resume	135
resumption	17

retail	34
retailer	35
retired	53
retiree	53
retirement	52
retirement benefits	53
retirement pay	53
retiring	53
revenue	112
revenue growth	113
revenue stamp	113
reverse	28
reversible	29
revolt	85
rise to the occasion	45
risk	24, 52
risk management	25
risky	25
rollaway	64
roller coaster	65
romantic	85
romanticism	85
romanticist	85
romanticize	84

S

safe and sound	83
safe-deposit box	83
safety belt	83
safety device	213
sail	84
sailor	85
sales quota	27
sales representative	43, 137
satellite	41
satellite broadcasting	41
satellite television	41
scale back ~	116
scale up ~	117
scam	16
scamper	17
scan	17
scar	17
scratchy	151
screen	99
screening	98
seasonable	153
seasonal	151
seasoned	175

sector	106
secure	51
security	50
Security Council	51
security guard	51
security screening	51
seed	181
seedless	179
select	8
selection	9
selective	9
self-starter	133
sell *a person* down the river	47
sell like hot cakes	47
sell out ~	46
sell ~ short	47
serviceable	83
set the world on fire	67
sewage	193
shareholder	108
shell	180
shift	108
shift stick	109
shiftwork	109
shifty	109
ship	79, 130
shipment	78, 131, 185
shipping	131, 188
side effect	13, 151
sign	110
sign a contract (with ~)	31
signal	111
signatory	111
signature	111
silicon implant	13
simulate	96
simulated	97
simulation	97
slash	10
sleazy	217
slip *one's* mind	73
slip up	73
slippage	73
slippery	73
sloppy	73
Sloppy Joe	73
smart	57
smart card	56
snowball	101
snowbound	101

snowfall	100	stick	171
snowman	101	stimulate	97
snowstorm	101	stimulating	96
snowy	49	stimulation	97
sociable	59	stimulus	97
social security	59	stock	14
social studies	59	stock certificate	15
socialism	59	stock dividend	15
socialize	59	stock exchange	15
sole representative	45	stove	66
solely	45	strategic	115
solid	70	strategist	115
solidarity	71	strategy	114
solidify	71	strive	98
solidity	71	study session	55
soot	27	submission	213
sooty	27	submissive	213
southernmost	101	submit	210
sparkle	21	subscribe	177
sparkler	20	subscription	175
sparkling	21	substance	29
sparkling wine	21	substantial	28
specific	87	substantially	29
specifically	86	sue	15
specification	87	suffering	99
specify	87	suite	68
spill	193	sunbathe	77
spiritual	39	sunburn	77
spiritual song	39	sundries	76
spirituality	39	sundry	77
split *one's* sides	73	sunstroke	77
split the difference	73	suntan	77
spread	181	supervise	131
spreadable	179	supervision	131
sprig	179	supervisor	130
staff	167	supervisory	131
staff agency	168	supplement	171
staff training	168	supplementary	173
staff transfer	168	suppository	171
stake	50	surgeon	12
state	168	surgery	13
stated	168	surgical	13
statement	167	surplus	160
statistic	63	surrogate	22
statistical	63	surrogate mother	23
statistician	63	symptom	153
statistics	62	synthesis	107
steel	137, 193	synthesize	107
steelworker	139	synthesizer	107
steely	139	synthetic detergent	107

synthetic fabric	106
synthetic rubber	107

T

take a rain check	23
take a [the] risk	25
take effect	13
take ~ for granted	206
take in ~	9
take ~ in (one's) stride	9
take up with ~	9
tbsp.	179
telecommunicate	61
telecommunications	60
telecommute	61
telecommuting	61
teleconference	61
telegram	61
telegraph	61
telemarketing	61
teleshopping	61
televise	61
Ten Commandments	44
tendency	93
terminal	97, 213
terminal care	213
terminate	213
termination	97, 210
terminator	97
textile	86
the lost and found	49
theoretical	25
tickle	151
tide over ~	33
tidy	210
tine	180
tip	42, 105
tip off	43
tip-off	43
toll	77
tollbooth	77
toll-free	76
tool box	99
tool kit	99
tough	40
track	27
track and filed	27
track record	26
trade fair	209
transcribe	25
transcript	24
transcription	25
treatment	21
treaty	72
triangle	113
tricycle	113
trigger	151
trillion	113
trim	180
trimester	113
trio	113
trousers	117
trucking firm	185
trust	80
trustee	81
trustworthy	81
tuition	203
twins	113

U

unacceptable	167
under house arrest	63
underage	16
undercut	71, 177
underestimate	177
underlie	35
underlying	17
undermine	177
underpin	35, 70
underscore	35
undershirt	117
undershorts	117
understaffed	17
understate	71, 177
undertake	35
undervalue	175
underway	17
underwear	116
underwriter	35
unfold	181
union	92
unit	42
unit cost	43
unit price	11, 43
unlicensed	40
unlike	107
unlikelihood	107
unmitigated	209

unpredictable	219
upload	149
upstage	47
usage	163
U.S. - Japan Security Treaty	51

V

valid	60
validity	61
valuable	109
valuate	109, 177
valuation	109, 175
valuator	109, 177
value pricing	109
value-added	109
valueless	109
vase	218
virus	171
visual aids	114
visual telephone	115
visualization	115
visualize	115
visually	115
voluntarily	9
voluntary	9
voluntary [early] retirement	53
volunteer	8
vote	89

W

wage	92
weather forecast	105
web	23
website	22
wed	23
wedding reception	127
weekly	95
whale	8
whaler	9
whaling	9
when least expected	83
wholesale	10
wholesaler	11
winery	23
with respect to ～	81
withdraw	47
withstand	47
word processor	19

worldwide	67
write a good hand	77
wrong end foremost	91

Y

year-end	103
yearly	95, 103
yogurt	171

川村一代 （かわむら・かずよ）

三重県生まれ。三重大学教育学部卒業。在学中にミシガン州立大学へ文部省奨学生として留学。ミシガン州立大学大学院修士課程修了（M.A. in TESOL）。研究分野は語彙学習とタスク学習。関西外国語大学短期大学部助教授を経て、現在、皇學館大学文学部講師。三重大学非常勤講師。日本英語検定協会面接委員。
著書に『TOEICテスト990点満点達成のための英単語と英熟語』（こう書房）、『身によくつくTOEIC TEST完全攻略600点文法・語法』（共著、NOVA）、『大学生のTOEIC』（共著、朝日出版）、『英語のリスニングストラテジー』（共著、金星堂）、『総合英語パワーアップ 中級編』（共著、南雲堂）などがある。

【めざせ！600点→900点】
TOEIC®テスト解いて覚える英単語と英熟語

ⓒ K. Kawamura 2006
2006年 5月10日 初 版 発 行

著　者　　川　村　一　代
発行者　　鵜　野　健　二

発行所　こ　う　書　房

〒162-0805 東京都新宿区矢来町112 第2松下ビル
電話 03(3269)0581〈代表〉　　FAX 03(3269)0399
e-mail xla00660@nifty.ne.jp　url http://www.kou-shobo.co.jp/

印刷所■広研印刷　製本所■共栄社製本
Printed in Japan　定価はカバーに表示してあります。
ISBN4-7696-0901-9　C2082